# HOW TO REGISTER YOUR OWN TRADEMARK

*with forms*

Mark Warda
Attorney at Law

**Sourcebooks**
Inc.
Naperville, IL • Clearwater, FL

Second edition, 1997.

Published by: **Sourcebooks, Inc.**

<u>Naperville Office</u>
P.O. Box 372
Naperville, Illinois 60566
(630) 961-3900
FAX: 630-961-2168

<u>Clearwater Office</u>
P.O. Box 25
Clearwater, Florida 33757
(813) 587-0999
FAX: 813-586-5088

Cover Design: Andrew Sardina/Dominique Raccah, Sourcebooks, Inc.
Interior Design and Production: Andrew Sardina, Sourcebooks, Inc.

**Library of Congress Cataloging-in-Publication Data**
Warda, Mark
    How to register your own trademark : with forms / Mark Warda.—2nd ed.
       p.   cm.
    Includes index.
    ISBN 1-57071-226-3 (pbk.)
    1. Trademarks—Law and legislation—Southern States—Popular works.  2.  Trademarks—Law and legislation—United States—Popular works.  3. Trademarks—Law and legislation—United States—Forms.
    I.  Title.
KF3181.Z9W374      1997
346.7304'88—dc21
                                                                                      97-26625
                                                                                      CIP

Printed and bound in the United States of America.

Paperback — 10  9  8  7  6  5  4  3  2  1

# How to Register Your Own Trademark

# CONTENTS

# USING SELF-HELP
# LAW BOOKS

Whenever you shop for a product or service, you are faced with various levels of quality and price. In deciding what product or service to buy, you make a cost/value analysis on the basis of your willingness to pay and the quality you desire.

When buying a car, you decide whether you want transportation, comfort, status, or sex appeal. Accordingly, you decide among such choices as a Neon, a Lincoln, a Rolls Royce, or a Porsche. Before making a decision, you usually weigh the merits of each option against the cost.

When you get a headache, you can take a pain reliever (such as aspirin) or visit a medical specialist for a neurological examination. Given this choice, most people, of course, take a pain reliever, since it costs only pennies, whereas a medical examination costs hundreds of dollars and takes a lot of time. This is usually a logical choice because rarely is anything more than a pain reliever needed for a headache. But in some cases, a headache may indicate a brain tumor, and failing to see a specialist right away can result in complications. Should everyone with a headache go to a specialist? Of course not, but people treating their own illnesses must realize that they are betting on the basis of their cost/value analysis of the situation, they are taking the most logical option.

The same cost/value analysis must be made in deciding to do one's own legal work. Many legal situations are very straight forward, requiring a simple form and no complicated analysis. Anyone with a little intelligence and a book of instructions can handle the matter without outside help.

But there is always the chance that complications are involved that only an attorney would notice. To simplify the law into a book like this, several legal cases often must be condensed into a single sentence or paragraph. Otherwise, the book would be several hundred pages long and too complicated for most people. However, this simplification necessarily leaves out many details and nuances that would apply to special or unusual situations. Also, there are many ways to interpret most legal questions. Your case may come before a judge who disagrees with the analysis of our authors.

Therefore, in deciding to use a self-help law book and to do your own legal work, you must realize that you are making a cost/value analysis and deciding that the chance your case will not turn out to your satisfaction is outweighed by the money you will save in doing it yourself. Most people handling their own simple legal matters never have a problem, but occasionally people find that it ended up costing them more to have an attorney straighten out the situation than it would have if they had hired an attorney in the beginning. Keep this in mind while handling your case, and be sure to consult an attorney if you feel you might need further guidance.

# INTRODUCTION

A trademark can be the most valuable asset a business owns. Imagine what would happen if just anyone could call their soft drinks "Coca-Cola" or their hamburger restaurant "McDonald's." Those trademarks are worth millions of dollars in goodwill and repeat business to the companies that own them.

This book is being published during an exciting time for trademark owners. At the same time, Congress and the courts are expanding the rights of trademark owners, and the internet is expanding the uses of those rights. Meanwhile, trademark lawyers are filing registrations for new attributes of products, attempting to give to their clients even more rights.

The recently passed Federal Trademark Dilution Act now allows famous trademarks to keep even those in other fields from using similar marks. Decisions in recent court cases allow companies to stop others from producing goods that are similar in ways never before protected.

This year, trademark applications are up 20% and are expected to soon pass 200,000 a year. Even a "capitalist tool" like *Forbes* magazine has claimed that the law is getting out of control with one company winning a Supreme Court case protecting its "tacky Mexican" restaurant decor and another obtaining a trademark for pink color for insulation.

While commentators may be right to decry these changes as limiting the rights of other businesses, smart entrepreneurs should take advantage of the changes to be sure not to lose any rights if the changes are upheld.

It is the purpose of this book to explain in simple language the steps necessary to protect your trademark by properly registering it. Included are registration in the United States Patent and Trademark Office and in individual states. For years, the only books on the subject were legal treatises that were difficult even for lawyers to use. The first edition of this book was one of the first attempts to simplify this area of law for laymen.

It is advisable to read this entire book before attempting to register your mark. The first chapter explains the things you need to know about what a trademark is and what rights it confers. Chapters 2 through 5 explain how to prepare for filing your application. If you have not yet used your mark, you should use chapters 6 through 8 to register it. If you have already used it, then use chapters 7 through 9.

In most cases, the registration of a simple trademark should go smoothly. If for any reason your application becomes complicated, you are urged to consult one of the treatises or an attorney who specializes in trademark law. Some good trademark books are listed in the bibliography to this text, but others may also be available at your local law library. Many of them do an excellent job of explaining each step in the complicated actions such as fighting an opposition to your application.

Occasionally, a company using a similar mark that learns of your application may threaten a lawsuit in Federal District Court for infringement of their mark. In such a case, unless you are willing to abandon the mark immediately, or dedicate much time to researching trademark law, it is advisable to work with a law firm specializing in trademark litigation to plan further strategy. This is explained in chapter 11.

# FLOWCHART FOR REGISTERING A FEDERAL TRADEMARK

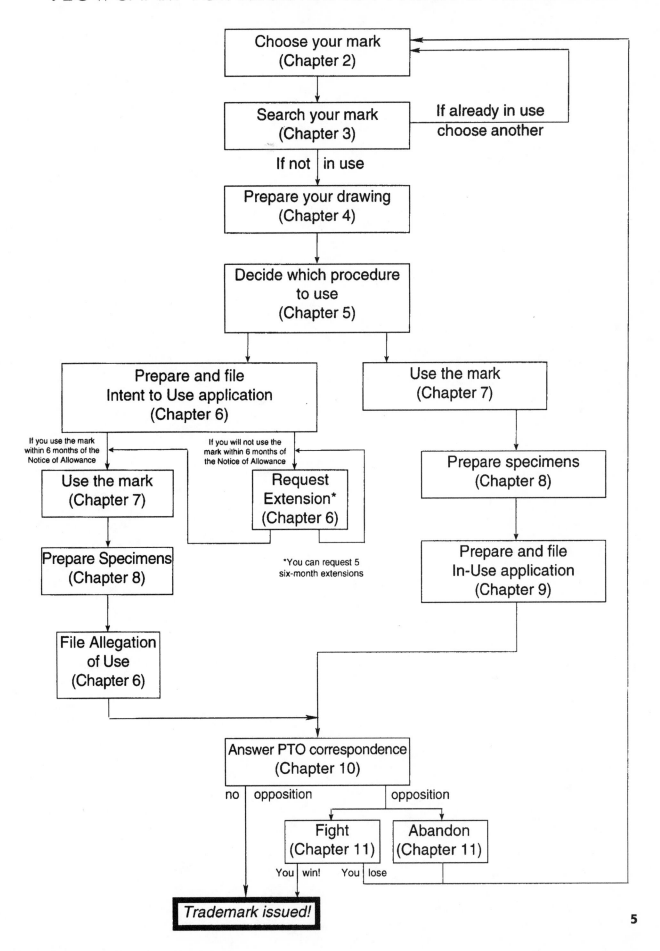

# TRADEMARK BASICS 1

## THE DIFFERENCES BETWEEN TRADEMARKS, COPYRIGHTS, PATENTS AND TRADE SECRETS

Even newspaper and magazine writers often confuse trademarks, copyright and patents. But these, along with trade secrets, are four completely different types of protections, usually used for completely different types of property, and protected in completely different ways. In order to obtain the right protection, you need to understand what each one protects.

PATENTS     A *patent* is protection given to new and useful inventions, discoveries and designs. A work must be completely new and "unobvious" to be entitled to a patent. A patent is granted to the first inventor who files for the patent. Once an invention is patented, no one else can make use of that invention, even if they discover it independently after a lifetime of research. A patent protects an invention for 17 years; for designs it is 3½, 7 or 14 years. Patents cannot be renewed. The patent application must clearly explain how to make the invention so that when the patent expires, others will be able to freely make and use the invention. Patents are registered with the United States Patent and Trademark Office (PTO). Examples of patentable things would be mechanical devices or new drug formulas.

**COPYRIGHTS**

A *copyright* is protection given to "original works of authorship" such as written works, musical works, visual works, performance works, or computer software programs. You cannot copyright titles, names, slogans, or works that have not been fixed in tangible form. A copyright gives the author and his heirs exclusive right to his work for the life of the author plus fifty years. Copyrights are registered with the Register of Copyrights at the Library of Congress. Examples of works that would be copyrightable are books, paintings, sculptures, songs, poems, plays, drawings, and films.

**TRADEMARKS**

A *trademark* is protection given to a name or symbol that is used to distinguish one person's goods or services from those of others. It can consist of letters, numerals, packaging, labeling, musical notes, colors, or a combination of these. A trademark lasts indefinitely if it is used continuously and renewed properly. Trademarks are registered with the United States Patent and Trademark Office. Examples of trademarks are the "Chrysler" name on automobiles, the red border on TIME magazine and the shape of the Coca-Cola bottle.

**TRADE SECRETS**

A *trade secret* is some information or process that provides a commercial advantage that is protected by keeping it a secret. Examples of trade secrets are a list of successful distributors, the formula for Coca-Cola, or a unique source code in a computer program. Trade secrets are not registered anywhere—they are protected by the fact that they are not disclosed. They are protected only for as long as they are kept secret. If you independently discover the formula for Coca-Cola tomorrow, you can freely market it. (But you can't use the trademark "Coca-Cola" on your product to market it.)

**UNPROTECTABLE**

Some things are just unprotectable. Such things as: ideas, systems and discoveries are not allowed any protection under any law. If you have a great idea, such as selling packets of hangover medicine in bars, you can't stop others from doing the same thing. If you invent a new medicine, you can patent it; if you pick a distinctive name for it, you can register it as a trademark; if you create a unique picture or instructions for the package, you can copyright them. But you cannot stop others from using your basic business idea of marketing hangover medicine in bars.

Notice the subtle differences between the protective systems available. If you invent something two days after someone else does, you cannot even use it yourself if the other person has patented it. But if you write the same poem as someone else, and neither of you copied the other, both of you can copyright the poem. If you patent something, you can have the exclusive rights to it for 17 years, but you must disclose how others can make it after the 17 years are up; however, if you keep it a trade secret, you have exclusive rights as long as no one learns the secret.

The following chart compares the important differences.

|  | Trademarks | Patents | Copyrights | Trade Secrets |
|---|---|---|---|---|
| **Works Protected** | Names or Symbols | Useful inventions, discoveries and designs | Written, visual musical or performance | Information or process |
| **Requirements** | Designation of origin | New and unobvious | Original work | Kept secret |
| **Claimant** | User | Inventor | Author | Owner |
| **Duration** | Unlimited if renewed | 17 years | Life of the author plus 50 yrs. | Unlimited if kept secret |
| **Protection if not registered** | Yes | No | Yes | Yes |
| **State Protection** | Yes | No | No | Yes |

# TRADEMARK TERMS

Before attempting to use or register a trademark, it is important to understand the various terms that are used and the legal distinctions between them. The word "trademark" is used generally to describe several types of marks. These different types of marks are used for different purposes and, in some cases, different application forms are needed for registering them.

TRADEMARK

A *trademark* is a word, name, symbol or device (or any combination thereof) that someone uses on his or her goods to distinguish them from others' goods. "Trademark" is not the proper term when referring to a name, symbol or device used in connection with services.

SERVICE MARK

A *service mark* is a trademark that is used in connection with services rather than goods. A service mark would apply to restaurant services, data services, or any other type of business that sells services rather than products. A restaurant (which is a service business) can also get trademarks on some of its products, such as the name Big Mac for a hamburger.

COLLECTIVE MARK

A *collective mark* is a word, name, symbol or device (or any combination thereof) that is used by members of a group such as a union, trade association, or cooperative. For example, unions use the little "union bug" symbol to designate products made by their members.

CERTIFICATION MARK

A *certification mark* is a symbol indicating that goods or services meet certain criteria such as purity or approval. It is usually owned by one organization and licensed to manufacturers to use on their products. The Good Housekeeping Seal of Approval, the UL label, and the Real symbol on foods are examples of certification marks.

TRADE DRESS

A *trade dress* is an overall look of a product or company that is distinctive and identifies that product. Trade dress usually involves shape and color such as the Coca-Cola bottle or the red border on TIME magazine.

TRADE NAME | A *Trade Name*, the name used for a business, cannot be registered as a federal trademark, because trademarks only apply to specific goods and services, not to company names. One way that a trade name can be protected is if it is registered as a trademark on goods, or a service mark on services, *and* used as a trade name. Another way trade names can be protected is through state law principles of unfair competition. See chapter 15 regarding other protection.

IN COMMERCE | In order to qualify for federal registration a mark must have been used *in commerce*, which means in business dealings across state lines or with someone in a foreign country. For a small restaurant that wants to protect its name, this can require interstate advertising. This requirement is explained in more detail in chapter 7. If your business will be purely local and you will never want to expand to another state or to franchise the business, you do not need federal registration of your trademark. Chapter 14 explains how to register your mark in your state.

CLASSES | Goods and services are divided into classes, and marks are registered according to the class into which the goods and services fall. If you will use your mark on goods or services that fall into different classes, then you will have to register the mark in each class in order to protect it. For each class you will have to pay an additional filing fee (presently $245; to find out if the fee has changed call 703-557-4636).

## TRADEMARK PROTECTIONS

There are three types of legal protections available for trademarks: common law, federal and state.

COMMON LAW | The *common law* is the body of law contained in judges' decisions rendered over the centuries based upon societal principles of justice. Some of these principles protect businesses from others that take unfair commercial advantage of their name or products. Because common law protection is based upon court decisions, it varies from state to state. You do not have to register anywhere for common law protection. If you are legitimately using a name, you are automatically granted certain rights just by using the name.

The basic principle of most of these laws is that someone may not "palm off" his goods as those of someone else, or misappropriate the efforts of others. What courts look for is a likelihood of customer confusion, which is against the public interest. It is not enough that two companies are competing for the same customers. There is nothing wrong with focusing on a profitable market segment and offering an alternative product. What you cannot do is fool the public into thinking your products are those of someone else.

Unfair competition law is often used to protect trade names that are not entitled to trademark registration. That is, if a company adopts a name that is similar to another's name, and if the similarity causes customer confusion, then a court may forbid further use of the name. In some cases, a person may be prohibited from using his own name to market a product. For example, a person named Joe Rolex would not be able to sell watches using his last name.

FEDERAL
TRADEMARK LAW

Federal trademark law is contained in the Lanham Act and is the main focus of chapters 5 through 13 of this book. It offers the broadest protection for trademarks used in the United States.

STATE
TRADEMARK LAW

State trademark laws have been passed by all of the states in the U. S. Unlike patents and copyrights, which are exclusively controlled by the federal government, trademarks may be registered with each state. The state laws offer simpler and less expensive registration, but the protection is limited to that state. If you plan to operate only a local business, you might want to consider state registration. More information is included in chapter 14.

# TYPES OF MARKS

Different types of marks are entitled to be registered. These are:

WORDS
Words such as Kodak, Microsoft, Netscape or Omega.

SYMBOLS
Symbols such as the big red K used by Kellogg; the pentagon used by Chrysler; or the Jolly Green Giant figure.

NAMES
Names such as McDonald's, Chevrolet or Templeton.

NUMERALS
Numerals or numeral combinations with letters or words, such as 747, Seagram's 7, or WD-40.

LETTERS
Letters, such as RCA for Radio Corporation of America, IBM for International Business Machines, or AA for American Airlines.

PACKAGING
Packaging, such as the shape of the Coca-Cola or Pierre Cardin cologne bottles. Recently companies have attempted to trademark the shape of a car as a trademark.

LABELING
Labeling, such as the red and white design on the Coca-Cola can.

SOUNDS
Sounds, such as the three musical notes used by NBC. Harley-Davidson is trying to trademark the sound of its motorcycle engines.

COLORS
Color, such as the pink color of certain fiberglass building insulation. Color is a difficult thing to trademark because there are a limited number of primary colors and if each company takes one, there will soon not be enough for new companies wanting to enter the field. Also, color cannot be trademarked if it is functional, that is, if the color is in some way important to use of the product. For example, a company that sold surgical instruments tried to trademark the color gray for its packaging. It lost because the court found that the color gray is useful as a background color to highlight the features of products in catalogs. *Specialty Surgical Instrumentation v. Phillips*, 30 U.S.P.Q.2d 1481 (8th Cir. 1994). However, in 1995 the U. S. Supreme Court ruled that a color can be trademarked if over time it has clearly become identified with a certain

brand. *Qualitex Co. v. Jacobson Products Co., Inc.,* 115 S. Ct. 1300 (1995).

COMPOSITES     Composites of two or more of the above features, such as a Coke bottle in the registered shape with the registered logo in the registered colors.

LOOK AND FEEL     The "look and feel" of a product is a relatively recent attribute to obtain protection. Look and feel can include the interface of a computer program, the design of a sweater, or the ambiance of a restaurant. A recent case even held that the design of a golf course can be protected by a "look and feel" trademark and another course could not copy its layout.

NEW TRADEMARKS     In addition to the above, companies are trying to trademark new things such as the moving image of a company logo at the beginning of a movie. As the value of trademarks grows in the new information age, expect trademark law to also expand significantly.

# TRADE DRESS

Trade dress is an expanding area of trademark rights. In recent years lawyers have argued, and judges have accepted, that such things as clothing designs, computer interfaces and even golf course layouts can be protected from infringement by trademark law. Today, attorneys are attempting to push the protection even farther, claiming trademark protection for such things as a unique play used in a sporting event.

In a 1992 case, the U. S. Supreme Court took this to somewhat of an extreme. In that case, a restaurant chain sued another for copying its "tacky Mexican" decor. The decor was not even trademarked but the chain claimed that it was a distinctive look and that people identified their restaurant by that look. The Supreme Court bought it and said that an unregistered trade dress of a restaurant can be protected from others who would copy it. *Two Pesos v. Taco Cabana, Inc.,* 505 U.S. 763, 112 S.Ct. 2753 (1992).

This is not a good situation for a supposedly free market. Rather than lower its prices to fight competition, a large business can take a smaller one to court and force them to stop making a product that is too similar to theirs.

Large companies can fight back. In two recent cases, businesses tried to stop competitors from making competing flower pots and child carriers, and they convinced the federal court they had a right to do so. Fortunately the competitors had the money to appeal, and the rulings were reversed. But how many small companies don't have money for legal battles and just give up? How many small businesses were forced to stop using names like "Insurance R Us" before Toys R Us had any right to control other areas besides toys, just because they couldn't afford to fight?

A more recent case indicates, however, that the important factor in deciding whether protection is given is not protection of the trademark owner, but protection of consumers from confusion. In this case, the maker of Vaseline Intensive Care Lotion came out with a new bottle and label for its product. A discounter copied the shape of the bottle as well as the colors and label, but also included its own logo and a notice that the product should be "compared to Vaseline Intensive Care Lotion." The court ruled that consumers would not be confused that it was the Vaseline product and that it was therefore not illegal. *Conopco v. May Dept. Stores*, 46 F 3rd 1556 (Fed. Cir. 1994). As one commentator put it, the decision struck terror into the hearts of trademark lawyers.

If you have a unique creation that you are not sure is protectable, consider fitting it into one of the trademark categories.

However, understand that this is one of the most confused areas of trademark law. Consider that after the Supreme Court's decision on Mexican restaurants, some circuit courts ignored it and made up their own test, other circuits criticized them, and district court judges criticized circuit court opinions. So if federal judges can't make up their minds on what the law is, there is little chance even the best lawyer will know.

The bottom line is, try to get as wide a trademark as you can, but be prepared for an expensive legal battle if a larger company goes after you.

# DOMAIN NAMES

The law of domain names has not yet been determined, but there are court cases pending at this moment that will begin to shape those rights. Domain names are the "addresses" of company sites on the internet. For example, to find the site of the New York Times, you would go to www.nytimes.com. Companies that wanted to use or reserve a specific name needed only to pay $100 and register it with Network Solutions, Inc., a company that was licensed by the U. S. Government's National Science Foundation.

Early in the development of the internet, certain people in the computer industry who saw the importance of domain name rights to major corporations registered as many names as they could think of that might be important to some corporation. Some invested as much as hundreds of thousands of dollars to register thousands of names.

In some cases this worked, and when companies finally decided to set up a web site and found that the name they wanted most was taken, they paid the original registrant for the rights.

But at least one company decided to fight the registrant. Intermatic, Inc. is the owner of a trademark "intermatic" for electrical timing devices. When it attempted to register "intermatic.com" as its domain name, it found that a Mr. Toeppen had already done so. In fact, Mr. Toeppen had registered about 240 domain names including such names as "nieman-marcus.com," "britishairways.com" and "ussteel.com." Rather than purchase the name from Mr. Toeppen, Intermatic sued claiming that his use was in infringement of their trademark. While there was no statute covering domain names, no clear precedent in the case law and no proof that Mr. Toeppen had actually used the trademark in a commercial way, the court analyzed the situation in a 32 page opinion. The court decided that use of a domain name is commercial in and of itself, and ordered Mr. Toeppen to hand over the domain name to Intermatic. *Intermatic, Inc. v. Toeppen*, 40 U.S.P.Q.2d 1412, 96 Civ. 1982 (N.D. Ill. 1996).

In the meantime, the contract with NSI has not been renewed and over 80 organizations are cooperating to develop a new domain name policy. In mid 1997 they agreed to create seven new generic top level domains (gTLDs) and to set up at least 28 new registrars around the world to accept registrations. The new gTLDs will be .firm, .store, .web, .arts, .rec, .nom, and .info. This is just the beginning, as even more gTLD names are expected in the future, and eventually .com will just be one of many possible addresses.

This will most likely free up a great number of names, since companies like Mcdonald's are not in the arts business and others should be able to use similar names in other fields. However, if large companies use dilution law, they may be able to keep others from using their name in other fields. (See the section on TRADEMARK DILUTION, page 21.)

# TYPES OF FEDERAL REGISTRATION

The Patent and Trademark Office maintains two different registers of trademarks, the Principal Register and the Supplemental Register.

THE PRINCIPAL REGISTER — The *Principal Register* is the one that provides all of the legal rights explained under REASONS FOR REGISTERING A TRADEMARK that follows.

THE SUPPLEMENTAL REGISTER — The *Supplemental Register* is used for marks that cannot be registered in the Principal Register because they are descriptive, geographic or surnames. Registration on the Supplemental Register prevents federal registration of the mark by others and can sometimes be used to later register on the Principal Register if the mark becomes distinctive. Other than this, it does not offer much protection.

Sometimes, to rescue an application that is not acceptable on the Principal Register, it is possible to amend the application to seek registration on the Supplemental Register.

## FORBIDDEN TRADEMARKS

Certain marks may not legally be registered, and it is a waste of time and money to try. Some that are forbidden are:

GENERIC

Generic names are names that merely describe a product. For example, Blue-Denim Jeans could not be registered since it describes a product. But you could call your product "Klondike Blue Denim Jeans" and register the name "Klondike." 15 U.S.C. §1127.

IMMORAL OR SCANDALOUS

*Immoral* or *scandalous* have been defined to include things that are shocking to the sense of propriety, offensive to the conscience or moral feelings, calling out for condemnation, vulgar, lacking in taste, indelicate or morally crude. For example, a photograph of a nude couple embracing and kissing was rejected, as was the mark "Bullshit." However, "Weekend Sex" was accepted for the name of a magazine, and "Big Pecker Brand" was acceptable as a trademark for T-shirts since it included the picture of a bird which "would make it less likely that purchasers would attribute any vulgar connotation to the mark." 15 U.S.C. §1052(a).

FALSE CONNECTION

A mark may not falsely suggest a connection to a person or institution. Besides being unregisterable, using someone's name on a product would violate their right to privacy for which they could sue for damages. Even using a person's nickname or other designation could be a problem. Chi-Chi's restaurants were sued by Jimmy Buffett for using the term "Margaritaville" for which he was known. 15 U.S.C. §1052(a).

**DECEPTIVE**  A mark may not be deceptive. For example, "Lovee Lamb" was deceptive when used on seat covers not made of lambskin, "Perry New York" was deceptive when used on clothing originating in North Carolina, and "American Limoges" was deceptive when used on dinnerware neither from Limoges, France, nor made from Limoges clay. However, the mark "Sweden" was acceptable for artificial kidney machines though they were not made in Sweden because the deception was held to be "perfectly innocent, harmless or innocent." 15 U.S.C. §1052(a).

**DISPARAGING**  Marks that disparage a person, institution, belief or national symbol are not registrable. It is not a problem to use a national symbol, only to use it disparagingly. National symbols have been held to include such things as the bald eagle and hammer and sickle (however since the collapse of the Soviet Union, the hammer and sickle may now be available, though perhaps not valuable, as a trademark). Things such as the "House of Windsor," the space shuttle, or the Boston tea party have been held not to be national symbols. 15 U.S.C. §1052(a).

**FLAGS, INSIGNIA COATS OF ARMS**  A private party may not trademark the flag, insignia or coat of arms of the United States or any state, municipality or foreign nation. Also forbidden is a simulation of any of these. Whether a mark simulates a flag or coat of arms depends upon the exact characteristics of each. An eagle in a triangular shield, not held to simulate the seal of the United States, and a globe with six indistinguishable flags were both acceptable. The letters USMC were held not to be an insignia and were allowed as a trademark, but a special law was passed to be sure that this wouldn't happen again. 15 U.S.C. §1052(b).

**NAME, PORTRAIT SIGNATURE**  One may not trademark the name, portrait or signature of a living person without his or her written consent, or of a deceased president of the United States during the lifetime of his widow without her written consent. For example, Steak and Ale Restaurants were not allowed to register "Prince Charles" as a brand of steak (even though there may be many persons with such a name), but Coca Cola was allowed to register the drink name "Fanta" over the objections of Robert D. Fanta. 15 U.S.C. §1052(c). (See chapter 2 for more comparisons.)

CONFUSINGLY SIMILAR

A mark may not be registered if it is confusingly similar to a registered mark or a mark previously used by another that has not been abandoned. Through your search, you may notice marks similar to your own. Even if they are not exactly the same as your mark, yours may be rejected if the examiner thinks that the public would be confused. Examples of marks that were too similar are, "Trucool" and "Turcool," "Commcash" and "Communicash," "Cresco" and "Kressco," "Entelec" and "Intelect," "Seycos" and "Seiko." Examples of marks that were held to be not confusing are, "Tia Maria" and "Aunt Mary's," "Best Jewelry" and "Jeweler's Best," and "Cobbler's Outlet" and "California Cobbler." 15 U.S.C. §1052(d).

GEOGRAPHIC

A mark may not be registered if it is primarily geographic. For example, you cannot register as a trademark the name "Georgia Peaches." But you could call your peaches "Sunshine Georgia Peaches" and register the word "Sunshine." 15 U.S.C. §1052(e).

SURNAMES

Unless a surname has acquired distinctiveness it may not be registered. This is because one person cannot establish exclusive rights to his surname until the public has begun to identify the name with the goods or services. One well-known surname which has acquired distinctiveness is Mcdonald's. 15 U.S.C. §1052(e)(3).

FUNCTIONAL FEATURES

If the feature of a product is functional, that feature may not be trademarked. This is so that competitors are not stopped from making the product. For example, Rolodex Corp. tried to trademark index cards with rounded corners and curved sides; and Bose Corp. tried to trademark a five-sided loudspeaker enclosure. Both were refused. 15 U.S.C. §§1051, 1052 and 1127.

ORNAMENTATION

Mere ornamentation that does not *distinguish* the goods from other goods may not be registered, since the point of a trademark is to distinguish goods or services. 15 U.S.C. §§1051, 1052 and 1127.

OLYMPIC

The word OLYMPIC and the Olympic logo were the subject of a special law passed by Congress. No one may use these even on an unrelated product or service. This law was upheld as constitutional by the U.S.

Supreme Court. *San Francisco Arts & Athletics, Inc. v. United States Olympic Committee*, 483 U.S. 522 (1987).

# TRADEMARK DILUTION

As explained earlier, a trademark is registered by class and only covers goods in one class. For example, in the past, the Ford Motor Company could not stop someone from using the trademark Ford for something unrelated—like bath oil beads. However, as corporations have expanded their operations into other fields and into other countries, they have sought to limit others' use of their marks.

A way companies have protected their marks from competitors in other fields is to claim that they *diluted* the value of their mark. Some states have laws which forbid uses which would dilute the value of a mark or tarnish its image. This theory only applies to famous marks that much of the population recognizes. For example, even though Coca-Cola is a registered trademark for beverages, if someone tried to sell "Coca-Cola" brand shoes they would probably be ordered by a court to stop, because they would be diluting the value of the mark to the Coca-Cola Company (and would confuse the public).

An important court case on this area of law is *Mead Data Central Inc. v. Toyota Motors Sales U.S.A. Inc.* 875 F. 2d 1026 (2d Cir. 1989). In that case, Mead sued Toyota to try to stop them from calling their new car Lexus because they said it would dilute the value of Mead's trademark Lexis for their legal information service. The district court ruled for Mead, but on appeal the decision was reversed. In a long and thoughtful decision, the court explained the law regarding dilution. The six factors that the court said were important in a dilution-by-blurring case are:

- ☞ similarity of the marks;
- ☞ similarity of the products;

> ☞ sophistication of the customers;

> ☞ predatory intent of the second mark's owner;

> ☞ renown of the first mark; and

> ☞ renown of the second mark.

**FEDERAL TRADEMARK DILUTION ACT OF 1995**

In 1995, Congress passed a law intended to give companies that own famous trademarks more protection from those who would use similar marks. This law allows companies to stop others from using marks that cause dilution of their marks regardless of whether the companies are in competition or whether there is consumer confusion. This is much greater protection than the law previously allowed.

However, despite the intent of the statute, most courts are still using the *Mead* test and requiring some basis for customer confusion.

Because the statute's protections may offer protections so broad that they violate the rights of others, the courts' limitations may be good in that they keep that act from being overbroad or even unconstitutional.

Here are a few examples of the results of the early cases under the law.

☞ Ringling Brothers sued a bar that billed itself as the "Greatest Bar on Earth" and the Utah Division of Travel Development for claiming it had the "Greatest Snow on Earth" claiming they diluted their mark "Greatest Show on Earth." Ringling lost both cases. However, years earlier, Ringling was able to stop a car dealer from advertising the "Greatest Used Car Show on Earth."

☞ American Express sued a company using the slogan "Don't Leave Home Without My Pocket Address Book," claiming it infringed its mark "Don't Leave Home Without It" and lost.

☞ Anheuser-Busch was able to stop a company from selling t-shirts with the logo "Buttwiser" on them.

☞ Toys "R" Us was able to stop a company from calling an adult-oriented web site "Adultsrus"

You may notice a pattern here. It appears that courts are less likely to allow a similar mark if the use appeals to prurient interests.

The important thing to remember when choosing your mark is that it should not be so similar to a famous mark that the owner of that mark will sue you. In a close case, where your products are different you may win, but can you afford a lengthy court fight with a major corporation? Of course if you have a family lawyer who would help you at a reduced rate, you might get a lot of publicity for your company by fighting a Goliath.

# REASONS FOR REGISTERING A TRADEMARK

A trademark is legally entitled to some protection even if it is not registered. As explained previously, the common law recognizes that a person who uses a distinctive mark on his goods is entitled to court protection from those who try to pass off their goods as theirs. However, the registration of a mark under federal law entitles the registrant to the following additional legal rights and benefits:

PRIORITY
The benefit of nationwide priority. Even if you are using the mark in only one area, registration gives you the right to the mark in every area of the country where it is not already being used.

CONSTRUCTIVE NOTICE
The benefit of *constructive notice*. This means that no one can say they didn't know you were using the mark. Registration officially notifies everyone in this country that you own the mark, whether they actually know it or not.

FEDERAL COURT
The right to sue in Federal District Courts for trademark infringement.

DAMAGES
The right to recover profits, triple damages, court costs and attorneys' fees in a court action.

CUSTOMS
The right to deposit the registration with the Customs service to stop the importation of goods that bear an infringing mark.

EVIDENCE OF
VALIDITY

The benefit of *prima facie* evidence of validity of your mark. This means that if you go to court, you don't have to waste time and money proving your ownership and exclusive right to use the mark.

INCONTESTABILITY

The benefit of possible incontestability, which means that the registration is conclusive evidence of your exclusive right to use the mark in commerce.

STRENGTH OF
MARK

The benefit of more limited grounds for attacking the registration once it is five years old.

CRIMINAL
PENALTIES

The benefit of having criminal penalties for those who may counterfeit your mark. The penalty may be up to $250,000 or five years for the first offense, $1,000,000 or fifteen years in prison for the second or subsequent offense.

FOREIGN
REGISTRATIONS

The benefit of having a basis for filing trademark applications in foreign countries.

In addition to the legal rights, the registration of a trademark confers some practical benefits:

ASSET

Registration makes the trademark a quantifiable asset that can more easily be licensed, sold, mortgaged or transferred.

TAX BENEFITS

Registration allows some tax benefits both for Federal income tax purposes and for some state tax purposes such as service taxes.

SALABLE

If a large company someday wishes to use your mark, they may offer to pay you for your rights in it.

## ACTIVITIES THAT ARE NOT PROTECTED

Although the owner of a trademark is guaranteed "exclusive use" of the mark, that right is limited as follows:

PREVIOUS USERS

Registering a mark does not allow you to stop others who have previously been using the mark. Persons who have used the mark prior to the person who registered it may continue to use it in the area where they have used it in the past. However, they may not expand their use to other areas of the United States once it has been registered by someone else.

CLASS     A registration only covers a specific class of goods. For example, if one company registered the mark Penguin for tuxedos, another company could register the same mark for ice cream bars.

OWNERS OF THE
PRODUCT     An owner of a product can use the trademark of the goods he is selling or leasing. If you own a Mercedes-Benz you can use that trademark to advertise and sell it.

COMPETITORS'
COMPARISONS     A competitor may use another person's registered mark in a comparison of the goods. For example, Carlton cigarettes can use the Camel cigarette trademark in an ad that states that Carlton has lower tar.

SCENES     Someone taking a photo or making a film of a scene comprising a variety of objects can include trademarked products without permission. For example, someone taking a photo of Times Square does not have to get permission for all of the trademarks visible in the scene. The reason for this is common sense—outdoor photographers would be out of business if they had to get permission for every mark in their photos. In reality, many trademark owners eagerly pay filmmakers to use their marks and this has become a big source of revenue for them. When you see Sylvester Stallone using a certain brand of cigarettes it is not because it is his normal brand, it is because a company paid well for the placement of its product in his film.

PARODIES     While trademark law does not contain the same specific permission for parody that copyright law does, First Amendment principles and the general confusion between copyright and trademark law have resulted in rulings that allow trademarks to be used in parodies. As the Seventh Circuit Court of Appeals noted, "When businesses seek the national spotlight, part of the territory includes accepting a certain amount of ridicule." *Nike, Inc. v. "Just Dit It" Enters.*, 6 F. 3d 1225 at 1227 (7th Cir. 1993).

# For Further Guidance

THE WEB    The United States Patent and Trademark Office has a website that includes a lot of useful material, including the latest rulings and revisions of forms. The address is http://www.uspto.gov/

TREATISES    For much more detailed explanation of the fine points of trademark law, a treatise on the subject would answer nearly any question. These are available at larger law libraries. The best law libraries are located at law schools and most are open to the public. See the books listed in the Bibliography.

TRADEMARK MANUAL    The *Trademark Manual of Examining Procedure* (TMEP) is the book used by government trademark attorneys to review your application. It answers nearly any question that could arise in the process. If your application is complicated or you want to know more of the details about the law, you should order a copy of it. It is available from the Superintendent of Documents. A new edition was released in 1997 at a price of $44.00. The order number is 903-010-00000-2. You can order it with a credit card by phone at 202-512-1800, by fax to 202-512-2250 or by mail from the following address:

> Superintendent of Documents
> P. O. Box 371954
> Pittsburgh, PA 15250-7954

# CHOOSING YOUR MARK 2

Before spending the money to search a mark and file your application for registration, you should take the time to carefully choose a mark that will be both practical and legal. You should have already read the previous sections on what types of marks are available (page 13) and what types of marks are forbidden, (page 18).

The two most important rules in choosing a mark are to be sure it is *not descriptive* and will *not cause confusion* with other marks. Other factors to consider are whether it is easy to remember, what images it evokes and, if you are exporting, what it means in foreign languages. (General Motors learned the importance of checking its marks in other languages when it realized that the name of its Nova model means "It doesn't go" in Spanish!)

## TYPES OF MARKS

There are four basic types of words that can be used to identify goods and services: coined, arbitrary, suggestive, and descriptive.

COINED    The best types of marks are those which are created and have no prior meaning. Kodak is a good example. The word had no meaning until Mr. Eastman started using it for his products. Therefore, it could not fall into any of the forbidden categories and no one else would have been using it. Another more recent example is Exxon, which was the new name adopted by the Esso company. Because Esso was doing business in so many countries, it wanted a mark that would be useful all over the world and not have any negative meaning. It used a computer to create the word Exxon and to be sure it had no prior meaning in any language in the world.

However, one drawback to using a newly coined word for a mark is the expense of teaching consumers what it means. Jaguar or LeBaron gives you an impression of what type of car you are supposed to be buying. If an automobile company started marketing a Qqueezoo car, what image would it inspire without a massive advertising campaign?

ARBITRARY The second best type of mark is one that is unrelated to the product, such as Domino's pizza or Peaches record stores. With such a mark, it is less likely that someone else is using the same mark on a similar product, and it is in no way descriptive of the product.

SUGGESTIVE A less advantageous type of mark is one that suggests the nature of the product. Examples of this would be Mr. Jiffy printing or Coppertone suntan lotion. People like to use these kinds of marks because they are easy to remember and often suggest that the goods have an advantageous quality. The disadvantage of using these over arbitrary and coined marks is that there is likely someone out there somewhere who is already using the mark.

DESCRIPTIVE The weakest mark would be one that is descriptive of the product. Examples would be Long Life batteries or Krispy crackers. If a mark is "merely descriptive" it won't even be registered unless it can be proved that after extensive use, the mark has acquired a secondary meaning. This means that a large number of persons identify with the applicant's product when they see the mark. Unless you have been using a descriptive mark for many years, you should not try to register it as a trademark.

# CHOOSING A MARK

Because a trademark is something that will identify your product and be used for the life of your business, you should choose it carefully. You should also come up with a list of possible marks, because with the millions of businesses in this country, it is likely that some of the marks you think are best are already taken.

If you are about to launch a blockbuster product or service that will take the nation by storm, or if you have a large marketing budget, then you can pick nearly any word to use as your mark. But if you would like your mark to help your product or service, it should be especially clever or distinctive so that people remember it.

An example of a cute name would be "curl up and dye" for a beauty parlor. A name like that would likely get mentioned in a local paper and perhaps even in a national publication. A slightly more obscure name such as "edifice wrecks" for a demolition company would get the attention of most people, but a large segment of the population just wouldn't get it.

Using a mark like Domino for a pizza restaurant or, even better, Subway for a submarine sandwich restaurant, opens up the possibility of using distinctive domino or subway graphics in the restaurant, its advertising, and promotional materials.

So, how do you choose a mark? Sit down with a dictionary, an encyclopedia and a thesaurus and start looking up words you like or that might work with your product. The creators of early page layout programs for the Macintosh named their company Aldus after an early pioneer in the printing field.

One way to expand possible trademarks is to use more than one word for your mark. For example, while you can't use Georgia or "peaches" alone as a trademark, you might want to use the mark "Sunshine Georgia Peaches" as a trademark. However, you will only be able to claim the word "sunshine" (since "Georgia" and "Peaches" cannot be registered, as explained in the last chapter). What you can do is use "Sunshine Georgia Peaches" as your mark and to disclaim any rights in the other two words. This is done by including in the application a statement such as, "No claim is made to the exclusive right to use 'Georgia' or 'peaches' apart from the mark as shown."

SOFTWARE
Computer software is available that is supposed to help the process of selecting a name. While it is pricey for a one-time use, you may wish to consider it if you need to name several products.

CONSULTANTS
There are consultants who offer to help find an ideal trademark for a fee, however the fee is often a lot more than a small business can afford. A business magazine once ran a story about a major corporation that paid $50,000 for a company to come up with a name for their new breakfast cereal. The magazine also polled its own staff for suggestions based on the criteria given to the consultant and came up with the same name!

## USING A STYLIZED TRADEMARK

Besides the basic word that usually constitutes a trademark, a stylized mark or logo may be registered. The advantage is that you can keep others from using similar designs, the disadvantage is that they may be able to use a similar word in a different style and not be found to be confusing.

## SIMILAR MARKS

NATIONAL
BRANDS
With all the millions of businesses in this country, and the countless products and services produced by each, it is unlikely that your mark will be unique and not in use by anyone. The question is, how similar should your mark be to another mark.

Unless you think you can benefit from a David and Goliath lawsuit with a major corporation (and can afford it) you should not use a mark that is similar to a nationally known brand. The new federal anti-dilution statute gives owners of famous brands the power to stop others whose marks come close to theirs. You may not get noticed by a major company for several years, but if they do come after you after you have been using a mark for several years, it may be very expensive to make a change. So avoid a mark that looks like a national brand.

# EXAMPLES OF SIMILAR MARKS THAT HAVE BEEN REJECTED

One of the following was rejected because the other already existed.

• CONFIRM for blood gas analyzer and CONFIRMCELLS for diagnostic blood reagents.

• LAREDO for land vehicles and LAREDO for pneumatic tires.

• BIGG'S for a grocery and general merchandise store and BIGGS for furniture.

• GOLDEN GRIDDLE for pancake house restaurant and GOLDEN GRIDDLE for table syrup.

• MUCKY DUCK for mustard and THE MUCKY DUCK for restaurant.

• CAREER IMAGE for women's clothing and CREST CAREER IMAGES for uniforms.

• 21 CLUB for clothing and THE "21" CLUB for restaurant services and towels.

• VEGETABLE SVELTES for wheat crackers and SVELTE for frozen desert.

• SPRAYZON for industrial cleansers and SPRA-ON for furniture cleaner.

• RESPONSE for banking services and RESPONSE CARD for 24 hour bank card.

• SEYCOS for watches and SEIKO for watches.

• CAYNA for soft drinks and CANA for fruit and vegetable juices.

• BUENOS DIAS for bar soap and GOOD MORNING for latherless shaving cream.

• LUPO for men's and boys' underwear and WOLF for clothing.

• RUST BUSTER for rust penetrating spray and BUST RUST for penetrating oil.

# EXAMPLES OF SIMILAR MARKS THAT HAVE BEEN ACCEPTED

• LITTLE PLUMBER for liquid drain opener and LITTLE PLUMBER for advertising services.

• CATFISH BOBBERS for fish and BOBBER for restaurant services.

• GOLDEN CRUST for flour and ADOLPH'S GOLD'N CRUST for food coatings.

• DESIGNERS/FABRIC for fabric store and DAN RIVER DESIGNER FABRIC for textile fabrics.

• CROSS-OVER for bras and CROSSOVER for ladies' sportswear.

• BOTTOMS UP for ladies' and children's underwear and BOTTOMS UP for men's clothing.

• PLAYERS for men's underwear and PLAYERS for shoes.

• REPECHARGE for skin care products and SECOND CHANCE for toiletries.

• TIA MARIA for restaurant services and AUNT MARY'S for canned fruits and vegetables.

• HAUTE MODE for hair coloring and HI-FASHION for finger nail enamel.

• BEST JEWELRY for jewelry store and JEWELER'S BEST for jewelry.

• BED & BREAKFAST REGISTRY and BED & BREAKFAST INTERNATIONAL both for lodging reservations.

• COBBLER'S OUTLET for shoes and CALIFORNIA COBBLER for shoes.

• ASO QUANTUM for laboratory reagents and QUANTUM 1 for laboratory instrument.

You may notice that there does not seem to be much difference between the ones that are acceptable and the ones that are not. You have just learned what law students study for three years: There is no absolute answer in law, and any case can go either way depending on the judge, the parties, the lawyers and the jury.

The lesson in this is, don't choose a mark that might be found to be confusingly similar to another mark, especially when the other company is bigger than yours.

## CHOOSING THE CLASSIFICATION

Prior to searching your mark, you need to decide the classes into which your goods or services fall. If your goods are related, such as beers, waters and sodas, then they will all fall into the same class. However, if you plan to use one mark on such different items as perfume, clothing and jewelry, then you will have to do a separate search and file a separate application for each of these classes of goods. There will be a separate fee for each class both when you order your search and when you file your application.

Goods and services are classified according to a system of International classifications. Prior to September 1, 1973, the United States had a separate system of classifications. Because many marks from before 1973 are being renewed, it is advisable to list both systems of classifications on the application and drawing for your mark.

The International classes and the U.S. classes are listed in appendix A.

# Searching Your Mark 3

There is no requirement for a trademark search before filing your registration, but if your mark is rejected because it is too similar to an existing mark then you will not get your filing fee back.

Even if you are already using the mark, you should have a search done before filing your application. You can register your mark if someone else is using it, but not if they have registered it for the same type of goods you will be using it on.

If others are using the mark, even in limited areas, your registration will not affect their use of the mark. If enough others are using the mark, or something similar, then you may decide it would be better to choose another mark.

There are two types of searches you can do, a search of companies and products that use the mark, and a search of the trademark office for registrations of the mark.

## Preliminary Search

Before you spend the money on a trademark office search or a comprehensive search, you should make a preliminary search yourself. You can start your search in your local public library. Many libraries have the

*Thomas Register*, the *Trade Names Directory*, Yellow Pages of major cities and other reference books listing companies and products. Some libraries now have computers that can access trademark records. This way, some of the names can be eliminated before spending the money for a formal search.

If you have a computer with internet access, you can use it to search all of the yellow page listings in the U. S. at no charge at a number of sites. One that at the time of publication of this book offers free yellow pages searches of all states at once is: http://www.infoseek.com

No matter how thorough your search is, there is no guarantee that there is not a local user somewhere with rights to the mark. If, for example, you register a name for a new chain of restaurants and later find out that someone in Tucumcari, New Mexico, has been using the name longer than you have, that person will still have the right to use the name, but just in his local area. If you do not want his restaurant to cause confusion with your chain, you can try to buy him out. Similarly, if you are operating a small business under a unique name and a law firm in New York writes and offers to buy the rights to your name, you can assume that some large corporation wants to start a major expansion under that name.

## TRADEMARK RECORDS SEARCH

The most important type of search to be done is a search of the trademarks already registered. You can do the search yourself, or you can pay for a search by a company that specializes in such searches.

TRADEMARK OFFICE SEARCH

The search library of the Patent and Trademark Office is located on the second floor of the South Tower Building, 2900 Crystal Drive, Arlington, VA 22022. It is open to the public free of charge, Monday through Friday from 8:00 AM to 5:30 PM.

DEPOSITORY
LIBRARIES

In addition, there are over 70 patent and trademark depository libraries throughout the country. These libraries have CD-ROMS listing all registered and pending marks, but they do not contain images of design marks. A list of these libraries is located at the end of this chapter.

SEARCH
FIRMS

If you do not wish to take the time to do the search yourself, you can hire a company that specializes in search services. A few companies that provide these services are:

> Government Liaison Services, Inc.
> 3030 Clarendon Blvd., Suite 209
> P. O. Box 10648
> Arlington, VA 22210
> (800) 642-6564; (703) 524-8200
>
> Thomson & Thomson
> 500 Victory Road
> North Quincy, MA 02171-1545
> (800) 692-8833
>
> XL Corporate Service
> 62 White Street
> New York, NY 10013
> (800) 221-2972

A simple trademark office search is usually at least $100, but it may be much more if there are many similar marks (of which you will receive copies). A separate search of unregistered marks that are also in use around the country (called a *common law* search) can be done for a similar fee. This would typically include a search of 100 trade journals and white page telephone directories and 4800 yellow page directories.

With all of the thousands of companies and millions of products produced today, it is likely that something will be found somewhere that is similar to your proposed trademark. Often 20 or even 50 different marks will be found to be similar to yours. Some of these might be the exact mark used on a different type of product, or similar marks used on the exact product. You might be able to successfully register your trademark, or you might end up being sued by a large corporation. Whether you should abandon your proposed mark and come up with something different or stick with your original mark is a legal decision that is best made with the advice of an experienced trademark attorney.

However, even if you get the best trademark attorney in the country, there is no guaranty that his opinion will hold up if you are taken to court. Often, even federal judges with many years of experience are reversed by higher courts. This happened recently when Mead Data Central, owner of the Lexis legal research service, sued Toyota when it announced its new model would be called Lexus. Even though legal research services and cars are obviously in different classes of goods, and even though the marks were spelled differently, Mead argued that there would be confusion because both were sold to the same customers, lawyers. A federal judge bought the argument and forbid Toyota from using the Lexus name. Silly him. The appeals court reversed his decision and said that reasonable people would not be confused.

If your search does turn up a similar name on a similar product, it would be best not to use that name unless you have a trademark lawyer in the family who can handle your litigation. Trademark litigation costs an average of over $100,000. However, if a lot of money has already been invested in a name, or if it is important to your plans, you might want to take the chance. If the marks only have minor similarities or are in different classifications, you might not have any trouble. It is possible, too, that the other side might not contest your mark.

Also, you may contest another person's registered mark. The owner may not have filed the proper affidavit after five years to keep the registration effective, or he may have gone out of business, abandoned the mark, or otherwise acted improperly. If you wish to consider challenging a mark, you should consult an attorney who specializes in trademark law.

# PATENT AND TRADEMARK DEPOSITORY LIBRARIES

| | | |
|---|---|---|
| Alabama | Auburn University Library | (205) 844-1747 |
| | Birmingham Public Library | (205) 226-3680 |
| Alaska | Anchorage: Z.J. Loussac Public Library | (907) 562-7323 |
| Arizona | Tempe: Noble Library; Arizona State University | (602) 965-7010 |
| Arkansas | Little Rock: Arkansas State Library | (501) 682-2053 |
| California | Los Angeles Public Library | (213) 228-7220 |
| | Sacramento: California State Library | (916) 654-0069 |
| | San Diego Public Library | (619) 236-5813 |
| | San Francisco Public Library | (415) 557-4500 |
| | Sunnyvale Patent Clearinghouse | (408) 730-7290 |
| Colorado | Denver Public Library | (303) 640-6220 |
| Connecticut | New Haven: Science Park Library | (203) 786-5447 |
| Delaware | Newark: University of Delaware Library | (302) 831-2965 |
| Dist of Columbia | Howard University Libraries | (202) 806-7252 |
| Florida | Fort Lauderdale: Broward County Main Library | (954) 357-7444 |
| | Miami-Dade Public Library | (305) 375-2665 |
| | Orlando: University of Central FL Libraries | (407) 823-2562 |
| | Tampa: Tampa Campus Library, USF | (813) 974-2726 |
| Georgia | Atlanta: Price Gilbert Mem. Library, GIT | (404) 894-4508 |
| Hawaii | Honolulu: Hawaii State Public Library System | (808) 586-3477 |
| Idaho | Moscow: University of Idaho Library | (208) 885-6235 |
| Illinois | Chicago Public Library | (312) 747-4450 |
| | Springfield: Illinois State Library | (217) 782-5659 |
| Indiana | Indianapolis-Marion County Public Library | (317) 269-1741 |
| | West Lafayette: Purdue University Libraries | (317) 494-2873 |
| Iowa | Des Moines: State Library of Iowa | (515) 281-4118 |
| Kansas | Wichita: Ablah Library, Wichita State University | (316) 574-1611 |
| Kentucky | Louisville Free Public Library | (502) 561-5652 |
| Louisiana | Baton Rouge: Troy H. Middleton Library, LSU | (504) 388-2570 |
| Maryland | College Park: Engineering & Physical Sciences Library, University of Maryland | (301) 405-9157 |
| Massachusetts | Amherst: Physical Sciences Library, Univ. of MA | (413) 545-1370 |
| | Boston Public Library | (617) 536-5400 ext. 265 |
| Michigan | Ann Arbor: Engineering Transportation Library, University of Michigan | (313) 647-5735 |
| | Big Rapids: Abigail S. Timme Library Ferris State University | (616) 592-3602 |
| | Detroit Public Library | (313) 833-3379 |
| Minnesota | Minneapolis Public Library & Information Center | (612) 372-6570 |
| Mississippi | Jackson: Mississippi Library Commission | (601) 359-1036 |
| Missouri | Kansas City: Linda Hall Library | (816) 363-4600 |
| | St. Louis Public Library | (314) 241-2288 ext. 390 |
| Montana | Butte: Montana College of Mineral Science & Technology Library | (406) 496-4281 |
| Nebraska | Lincoln: Engineering Library Univ. of Nebraska | (402) 472-3411 |

| | | |
|---|---|---|
| Nevada | Reno: University of Nevada/Reno Library | (702) 784-6579 ext. 257 |
| New Hampshire | Durham: University of New Hampshire Library | (603) 271-2239 |
| New Jersey | Newark Public Library | (201) 733-7782 |
| | Piscataway: Library of Science & Medicine, Rutgers University | (908) 445-2895 |
| New Mexico | Albuquerque: Univ. of NM General Library | (505) 277-4412 |
| New York | Albany: New York State Library | (518) 474-5355 |
| | Buffalo and Erie County Public Library | (716) 858-7101 |
| | New York Public Library (the Research Library) | (212) 592-7000 |
| North Carolina | Raleigh: D.H. Hill Library, NC State University | (919) 515-3280 |
| North Dakota | Grand Forks: Chester Fritz Library, Univ. of ND | (701) 777-4888 |
| Ohio | Akron-Summit County Public Library | ((330) 643-9075 |
| | Cincinnati and Hamilton County, Public Library | (513) 369-6936 |
| | Cleveland Public Library | (216) 623-2870 |
| | Columbus: Ohio State University Library | (614) 292-6175 |
| | Toledo/Lucas County Public Library | (419) 259-5212 |
| Oklahoma | Stillwater: Oklahoma State Univ. Library | (405) 744-7086 |
| Oregon | Salem: Oregon State Library | (503) 768-6786 |
| Pennsylvania | Philadelphia, Free Library | (215) 686-5331 |
| | Pittsburgh, Carnegie Library | (412) 622-3138 |
| | University Park: Pattee Library, PSU | (814) 865-4861 |
| Puerto Rico | Mayaguez: General library, University of Puerto Rico | (787) 832-4040 ext. 4359 |
| Rhode Island | Providence Public Library | (401) 455-8027 |
| South Carolina | Clemson University Libraries | (864) 656-3024 |
| Tennessee | Memphis & Shelby County Public Library and Information Center | (901) 725-8877 |
| | Nashville: Stevenson Science Library Vanderbilt University | (615) 322-2717 |
| Texas | Austin: McKinney Engineering Library Univ. of Texas at Austin | (512) 495-4500 |
| | College Station: Sterling C. Evans Library, Texas A & M University | (409) 845-3826 |
| | Dallas Public Library | (214) 670-1468 |
| | Houston: The Fondren Library, Rice Univ. | (713) 527-8101 ext. 2587 |
| | Lubbock: Texas Tech Library | Not yet operational |
| Utah | Salt Lake City: Marriott Library, Univ. of UT | (801) 581-8394 |
| Vermont | Burlington: Bailey/Howe Library, University of Vermont | Not yet operational |
| Virginia | Richmond: James Branch Cabell Library Virginia Commonwealth Univ. | (804) 828-1104 |
| Washington | Seattle: Engineering Library, Univ. of WA | (206) 543-0740 |
| West Virginia | Morgantown: Evansdale Library, WV Univ. | (304) 293-2510 ext. 113 |
| Wisconsin | Madison: Kurt F. Wendt Library, Univ. of WI | (608) 262-6845 |
| | Milwaukee Public Library | (414) 286-3051 |
| Wyoming | Casper: Natrona County Public Library | (307) 237-4935 |

# Preparing Your Drawing 4

Once you have decided upon your mark, you must prepare the official drawing. If you are only seeking to register a word, this is simple since it can be merely typed in capital letters. It is not necessary to create a fancy style for your mark, but the drawing must be typed in a specific format. Also, if you use artwork, it must comply with strict rules.

For federal registration, the drawing of the mark must be in strict compliance with §2.52 of the *Rules of Practice in Trademark Cases*. One reason to register the mark in a specific style rather than typed is if you plan to use that style as an identifying symbol of your goods or services. Someone who uses a different name with the similar style may be held to be an infringer of your mark.

However, it is usually best to register the word alone, that way you can use those words in any configuration or style you choose.

The following are the requirements for the drawing:

1. Paper. *The drawing must be made upon paper which is flexible, strong, smooth, nonshiny, white and durable. A good grade of bond paper is suitable; however, water marks should not be prominent...The size of the sheet on which a drawing is made must be 8 to 8½ inches (20.3 to 21.6 cm.) wide and 11 inches (27.9 cm.) long. One of the shorter of the sheet should be regarded as its top.*

2. Heading. The drawing should comply strictly with the rules, even in the content and placement of the heading. *Across the top of the drawing, beginning one inch from the top edge and not exceeding one quarter of the sheet, list on separate lines applicant's name; post office address; date of first use; date of first use in commerce; and the goods or services recited in the application (or typical items of the goods or services if there are a large number). A typewritten heading is preferred.*

3. Special Form of Drawing. If the mark is stylized in any way, then the drawing must conform to the following:

*The drawing of the mark must be done in black ink, either with an india ink pen or by a process which will give satisfactory reproduction characteristics. Every line and letter, including words, must be black. This applies to all lines, including lines used for shading. Half-tones and gray are not acceptable. All lines must be clean, sharp, and solid, and not be fine or crowded. A printer's proof or camera ready copy may be used if otherwise suitable. Photographs are not acceptable. Photocopies are acceptable only if they produce an unusually clear and sharp black and white rendering. The use of white pigment to cover lines is not acceptable.*

*The preferred size of the drawing of the mark is $2\frac{1}{2}$" x $2\frac{1}{2}$", and in no case may it be larger than 4" x 4". If the amount of detail in the mark precludes clear reduction to the required 4" x 4" size, such detail should not be shown in the drawing but should be verbally described in the body of the application.*

*Where color is a feature of a mark, the color or colors may be designated in the drawing by the linings shown in the following chart:*

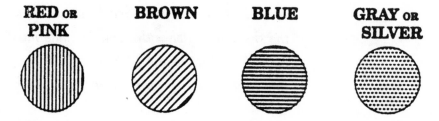

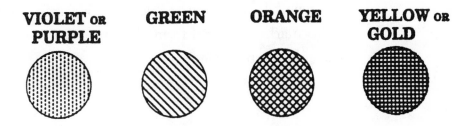

If the drawing contains these lines for color, a statement must also be included that explains which colors are designated by the lining.

If the mark is a drawing that is shaded, but not for color, then a statement should be included which indicates that the shading lines do not represent color (for example, "The lining shown in the mark is a feature of the mark and is not intended to indicate color").

If the mark is shaded for color, but you are not claiming the color to be part of your trademark, then a statement should be included which makes clear that you are not claiming rights to the color as part of the mark. For example, "but no claim is made to color," or "but color is not a feature of the mark."

If your stylized mark contains words that cannot be exclusively claimed, such as "Sunshine Georgia Peaches," you should disclaim rights to those extra words (for example, "No right is claimed to the exclusive right to use 'Georgia' or 'Peaches' apart from the mark as shown"). If your mark was not stylized, only the word "Sunshine" would be typed on your drawing.

If you use a typed drawing for your mark, you must only use characters that can be represented by pica or elite type. You can use the symbols, . ? " - ; ( ) % $ @ + , ! ' : / & # * = [ and ]. You cannot use symbols such as the degree symbol (°), subscripts, underlining or exponents. To do anything like this, you must use a stylized drawing.

If the mark is a sound or a scent, the drawing page should indicate "NO DRAWING" where the mark would otherwise appear.

A typed drawing may be folded as long as the fold does not run through the mark. A special-form drawing or any drawing on bristol board should not be folded.

## Sample Typed Drawing

APPLICANT'S NAME: Sphinx International, Inc.

APPLICANT'S ADDRESS: 1725 Clw/Largo Rd. Clearwater FL 33756

GOODS: Law books and legal forms

DATE OF FIRST USE: July 20, 1999

DATE OF FIRST USE IN COMMERCE: July 20, 1999

SPHINX

## Sample Stylized Drawing

APPLICANT'S NAME: Carol's Clothing, Inc.

APPLICANT'S ADDRESS: 1122 Ridge Rd. Anywhere, MT 01234

GOODS: Umbrellas, Women's slacks and blouses

FIRST USE: Umbrellas (Class 18) June 20, 1994
        Clothing (Class 25) January 29, 1994

FIRST USE IN COMMERCE:  Umbrellas (Class 18) June 20, 1994
                Clothing (Class 25) January 29, 1994

DESIGN:  A pointing hand

# CHOOSING THE PROCEDURE 5

Prior to November 17, 1989, a mark had to be in actual use in interstate or international commerce before an application for trademark could be filed. This was a problem for large companies that spent millions of dollars to market new products, because their money would be wasted if the mark was later rejected. To avoid this problem, companies would make a *token use* of the mark and then file the application. Token use usually meant shipping a sample product to a friend or relative in another state.

On November 17, 1989, the first major overhaul of the trademark law in forty years took effect. The biggest change was the new provision allowing Intent to Use applications. This procedure allows an application for a trademark to be filed by a person who has a "bona fide intent to use" a mark. The person then has six months to start using the mark after the application is filed. This six month period may be extended an additional six months without giving a reason, and an additional four more six-month extensions may be granted if good reason is given. Therefore, a person has a total of 3 years in which to make use of the mark.

Chapter 6 explains the procedure for filing an Intent to Use trademark application. If it will be a while before you can start legitimately using your mark, you should file an application as explained in chapter 6.

If you can quickly begin using your mark, or are already using it, you should skip chapter 6 and go right to chapters 7 and 8 which explain proper use of the mark and the type of specimens required. You can then file an application for a mark in use as explained in chapter 9.

As explained in chapter 7, token use is no longer allowed. The mark must be used in an actual transaction either after an Intent to Use application has been filed, or before a Use application is filed.

# Filing an Intent to Use Application

**6**

This chapter explains how to file your application for a trademark you have not yet used in interstate commerce, but for which you have a "bona fide intention" to use.

Because this procedure is relatively new, there is not a lot of legal guidance as to what constitutes proof of such an intention. However, in 1993 the Trademark Trial and Appeal Board made clear what is *not* a bona fide intention. In the case *Commodore Electronics Ltd. v. CBM Kabushiki Kaisha*, Commodore challenged CBM's application and asked CBM to produce proof that it intended to use the mark in all of the classes claimed. The Board ruled that a lack of any *documentation* proving an intent to use the mark is sufficient proof that there was no valid intention.

What type of documentation is necessary? A narrative of your plans dated and notarized prior to filing the application would be better than nothing. But the best documentation would be actual plans, memos and minutes of meetings explaining in detail the plans to use the mark.

The procedure for registering a mark that has not yet been used consists of two steps. The first step is to file an application along with a drawing of the mark and the filing fee at the Patent and Trademark Office. Then, after you have used the mark, you must send in three specimens of its use along with either an Amendment to Allege Use or a Statement of Use and an additional filing fee.

For an application to be valid, it must contain the following elements:

☞ The name and address of the applicant.

☞ The name and address of a person to whom communications can be addressed. (This is usually the applicant or his attorney.)

☞ A drawing of the mark.

☞ Identification of the goods or services on which the mark will be used.

☞ A claim that the applicant has a bona fide intent to use the mark in commerce.

☞ A verification or declaration paragraph.

# PREPARING THE APPLICATION

The easiest way to apply is to use the Patent and Trademark Office forms that are included in this book. However, it is also possible to type the information on white $8\frac{1}{2}$"x11" paper in the same style and layout as the sample application in appendix C of this book. Trademark rules prescribe the proper heading, margins, etc. ($1\frac{1}{2}$" margins at the top and left side, using only one side of the sheet).

To see if there is a more recent version of the form, you can check the United States Patent and Trademark Office website, and if necessary, download the form at: http://www.uspto.gov/web/fprms/

To show you how to fill in the forms, sample filled-in application forms are included in appendix B of this book. In addition, be sure to follow these instructions:

☞ The mark in the MARK box at the top should be the same as the drawing you submit.

☛ You are not required to fill in the "Class No." box; the Patent and Trademark Office will fill it in for you. However, you will already know the class from doing your search, so you might as well record it in case there is any chance for confusion. If you wish to register in more than one class, list them all here and be sure to pay a separate filing fee for each class.

☛ The applicant must be the owner of the mark who actually controls the nature and quality of the goods sold.

☛ Under "Goods and/or Services," you should use care in deciding on a description. The more narrowly you describe your claim, the more easily it will be approved, but the smaller your protection. For example, if you sell a blood test kit, you might want it to be considered a medical test kit so that no one else could use the mark on any type of medical test kit. If you claim the mark just for a blood test kit, then you will be less likely to conflict with other marks in the medical field that are similar.

☛ Under "Basis for Application," you should check the second box for an intent to use application. The third box is for those relying on a previous foreign application, and the fourth for those relying on a previous foreign registration.

☛ The date of first use in commerce and date of first use anywhere should be exact dates. If only a month and year are given, the last day of the month is presumed. If only a year is given, the last day of the year is presumed.

☛ The signature must be that of a proper party. For an individual, it must agree with the typed name of the applicant. For a partnership, it must be a signature of a general partner. For a corporation, it must be a signature of an officer holding an office established in the articles of incorporation. For example, if the person signing is designated "general manager" or "trademark manager," the application will probably be rejected. (For foreign applicants see chapter 13.)

ATTORNEYS

Attorneys who are filing for a client are reminded to add a clause appointing themselves to prosecute the application. This has been done in the typed application, but the same clause should be added to the prepared forms.

## SENDING IT IN

A completed application consists of the application itself, the drawing, and one application fee for each class in which the mark is to be registered. (As this book was going to press the fee was $245, but there are regular calls to raise it.) You should write or call the Patent and Trademark Office to confirm the current fee before filing your application. If you send the wrong fee it will be sent back, which will delay your filing date. The phone number is (703) 308-4357. The address is:

> Assistant Commissioner of Patents and Trademarks
> 2900 Crystal Drive
> Arlington, VA 22202-3513

Your application package should be sent in by certified mail, return receipt requested. If you send in your package by Express Mail and properly fill in the Express Mail number on your application, the date you mail it will be considered your filing date (unless that day is Saturday, Sunday or a Federal holiday in the District of Columbia). The necessary wording is on the application forms in this book. If you type your application, you must use this same wording.

After the application has been sent in, it will be reviewed for errors and published in the *Official Gazette*. These procedures are explained in chapters 10 and 11 of this book.

# STEP TWO IN INTENT TO USE APPLICATIONS

Prior to final registration of a mark, an Intent to Use applicant must use the mark in commerce and must file either an Amendment to Allege Use or a Statement of Use along with specimens and an additional filing fee. These used to be two separate forms but now one form, the Allegation of Use for Intent-to-Use Application, covers both situations. This form will be considered an Amendment to Allege Use or a Statement of Use depending upon when it is filed. A description of the proper type of use is explained in chapter 7, and an explanation of the proper specimens is included in chapter 8.

AMENDMENT TO
ALLEGE USE

The Amendment to Allege Use may be filed any time after filing the application and before the approval for publication in the Official Gazette. So, if you begin using the mark before it has been approved for publication, you should file an Amendment to Allege Use. A complete Amendment to Allege Use must contain the following:

☛ A verified statement that the applicant is believed to be the owner of the mark and that the mark is in use in commerce; the type of commerce; the date of the applicant's first use of the mark and first use of the mark in commerce; those goods or services specified in the application on or in connection with which the mark is in use in commerce and the mode or manner in which the mark is used.

☛ Three specimens of the mark as used in commerce.

☛ The filing fee of $100.

An Allegation of Use for Intent-to-Use Application form is included in this book as Form 7. As an alternative to using the included form, the information listed above may be typed on white $8\frac{1}{2}$"x11" paper and be titled "Amendment to Allege Use" at the top.

BLACKOUT
PERIOD

A blackout period exists between the approval for publication and the issuance of the Notice of Allowance. During which neither the Amendment to Allege Use nor the Statement of Use may be filed.

STATEMENT OF USE The Statement of Use may be filed after issuance of a Notice of Allowance. It must be filed within six months, unless an extension has been requested. This notice is issued after publication of the mark if there were no oppositions, or after any oppositions have been dealt with. The Statement of Use must contain the following:

☛ A verified statement that the applicant is believed to be the owner of the mark and that the mark is in use in commerce; the type of commerce, specifying the date of the applicant's first use of the mark and first use of the mark in commerce; those goods or services specified in the notice of allowance on or in connection with which the mark is in use in commerce and the mode or manner in which the mark is used.

☛ Three specimens of the mark as used in commerce.

☛ The filing fee of $100.

A form Allegation of Use for Intent-to-Use Application is included in this book as Form 7. As an alternative to using the included form, the information listed above may be typed on white 8½" x 11" paper and be titled "Statement of Use" at the top.

SIX-MONTH EXTENSION A six-month extension can be added to the initial six-month period for filing the Statement of Use. To obtain the extension, the applicant must file a Request For Extension during the initial six-month period. This form is included in this book as Form 8. Instead of using this form, the request may be typed on white 8½" x 11" paper. It must include the following:

☛ A verified statement signed by the applicant that the applicant has a continued bona fide intention to use the mark in commerce and a specification as to which goods or services the applicant intends to use the mark on.

☛ The fee of $100.

Up to four additional six-month extensions can be granted if the applicant can show good cause why it has not been possible yet to use the mark in commerce. To obtain the extension, the applicant must file a Request for Extension (as explained above) and include a statement showing a good reason for why the extension is necessary.

REQUEST TO
DIVIDE

If you have applied for a trademark on several classes of goods or services and only used it on some of the classes, you may divide your application and ask that the trademark be issued for the classes in use. Then you can get the trademark for the other classes at a later time, after you have used the mark on those classes.

To do so you must file a Request to Divide which is included in this book as Form 9.

A Request to Divide may be filed where the mark has been used on some of the intended goods, but not all. This way, a registration can be granted for the mark on some goods even if it will not be used on others until much later. A form for this purpose is included in this book.

# USING YOUR MARK 7

A trademark registration cannot be finalized until the mark has been *used in commerce*. Back when the law required a mark to be used before an application could be filed many applicants just made some token use of their mark, such as mailing a copy to a friend, in order to have a first date of use of the mark.

Because Intent to Use applications are now allowed, the requirements for actual use of the mark have been made more strict. Token use is no longer acceptable. Be sure to follow these rules in making use of your mark.

IN COMMERCE
One of the basic requirements for trademark registration is that the mark must have been used in commerce. *In commerce* is a legal term that means the mark must have been used in either interstate commerce or commerce with a foreign country. The specifics of the requirement are as follows:

1. The mark must have been affixed to the goods or the packaging, labels, or on tags on the goods. The mark should not be handwritten. It should appear there is an intention to make serious use of the mark as a trademark.

2. The product should be sold to an unrelated party at a normal price, and the product should not be returned nor the payment refunded.

The sale should be in the ordinary course of business and not just for the purpose of using the mark. It is best to have some sort of invoice or other written documentation of the sale.

SERVICE MARKS
When using service marks, such as for a restaurant where no goods are shipped across state lines, the mark must appear on advertising that is sent across state lines. The advertising should be for services that are currently available for sale, not merely an announcement of future availability.

COLLECTIVE MARK
To use a collective mark, such as the name of a club, the mark should be used on membership forms, stationery, etc.

CERTIFICATION MARK
A certification mark must be used by a party who is not the owner of the mark but whose products or services comply with the standards set for the mark. The owner of the mark must set definite standards for use of the mark and must be sure that users of the mark comply with the standards.

Prior to registration of a mark, you may claim ownership of a mark by using the symbol ™ next to your mark. If you are using a service mark, the symbol consists of the letters ℠. Even if you never register your mark with the Patent and Trademark Office, you can use these symbols to indicate your claim to ownership of a mark that you claim as a trademark on your goods or services.

If the mark has been registered in a foreign country, or if an application for registration has been filed in a foreign country, then use in commerce in the United States is not necessary. If relying on a foreign *application*, your U.S. application must be filed within six months of the foreign filing. If relying on a foreign *registration*, a certification or a certified copy of the foreign registration must be included.

# Preparing Your Specimens 8

Three specimens of the mark as actually used must be provided to the Trademark Office. These are either sent with the Present Use Application, or, if an Intent to Use Application is filed, they are sent with either the Amendment to Allege Use or the Statement of Use.

The specimens may be tags, labels, containers, displays or some similar use of the mark that can be arranged flat and are not larger than $8\frac{1}{2}$" by 11". Since the specimens need to be kept in your file at the Patent and Trademark Office, three dimensional or bulky specimens are not acceptable. If specimens complying with the above rules cannot be supplied (for example, if the mark is a metal ornament on an automobile or the shape of a bottle), three photographs of the mark may be submitted. The photographs must also be no larger than $8\frac{1}{2}$" by 11". The specimens may be identical or they may all be different.

Advertising materials are not acceptable as specimens for goods. Neither are instruction manuals, invoices, business stationery, nor bags used in a store at checkout. You must send actual labels or tags that are affixed to the goods. However, for services, such as a restaurant, advertising materials are acceptable. For marks that only appear on a video or television screen, a photograph of the screen with the mark displayed is acceptable.

If the trademark drawing is coded for specific colors on the mark, then the specimens must be in the correct colors.

The specimens must match the mark sought to be registered. If your drawing was typed, you can use any font style on your specimens, but the spelling should be identical.

If some material printed on the specimen is not in English, the examining attorney may require a translation of it "to permit a proper examination."

Since the symbol ® can only be used on a mark that has been registered, it should not be used on specimens of marks that you are in the process of applying for registration.

Only one specimen is necessary to receive a filing date, but two more must eventually be sent.

# FILING AN 9 APPLICATION FOR A MARK IN USE

If you have already used your mark in commerce, or if you can easily use your mark, then filing an Application for a Mark in Use is the best way to register it. It is easier and cheaper than filing an Intent to Use Application.

For a mark that has already been used in commerce, the following items are required for a complete application:

- ☞ the written application;
- ☞ the drawing of the mark;
- ☞ three specimens showing actual use of the mark; and
- ☞ the filing fee.

You should also include a self-addressed stamped envelope so that you will receive a receipt for your application.

## THE APPLICATION

For an application to be valid it must contain the following elements:

- ☞ The name and address of the applicant.

☞ The name and address of a person to whom communications can be addressed. (This is usually the applicant or his attorney.)

☞ The citizenship of the applicant.

☞ The classes in which the applicant wishes to register the mark. (See appendixes B and C for the listings of classes.)

☞ A statement that the applicant has adopted and is using the mark.

☞ A drawing of the mark

☞ Identification of the goods or services.

☞ A request that the mark be registered under the Trademark Act.

☞ The date on which the mark was first used in commerce.

☞ The type of commerce in which the mark was used (that is, interstate commerce or international commerce).

☞ The manner in which the mark is affixed to the goods or used to promote the services.

☞ If the applicant is represented by an attorney, then a statement should be included appointing the attorney to prosecute the application.

☞ An oath that the statements are true. This can be notarized or in the form of a *declaration*. The forms in this book use the declaration rather than notary.

The easiest way to file an Application for a Mark in Use is to use one of the Patent and Trademark Office forms that are included in this book. However, it is also possible to type the information on white 8½"x11" paper in the same style and layout as the sample application in appendix C of this book. Trademark rules prescribe the proper heading, margins, etc. (1½" margins at the top and left side, using only one side of the sheet).

To show you how to fill in the forms, sample filled-in application forms are included in appendix D of this book. In addition, be sure to follow these instructions:

☛ The mark in the MARK box at the top should be the same as the drawing you submit.

☛ You are not required to fill in the "Class No." box; the PTO will fill it in for you. However, you will already know the class from doing your search, so you might as well record it in case there is any chance for confusion. If you wish to register in more than one class, list them all here and be sure to pay a separate filing fee for each class.

☛ The applicant must be the owner of the mark who actually controls the nature and quality of the goods sold.

☛ Under "Goods and/or Services," you should use care in deciding on a description. The more specific you describe your claim—the easier it will be approved (but the smaller your protection). For example, if you sell a blood test kit, you might want it to be considered a medical test kit so that no one else could use the mark on any type of medical test kit. If you claim the mark just for a blood test kit, then you will be less likely to conflict with other marks in the medical field that are similar.

☛ Under "Basis for Application," you should check the first box for a mark already in use. The third box is for those relying on a previous foreign application and the fourth for those relying on a previous foreign registration.

☛ The date of first use in commerce and the date of first use anywhere should be exact dates. If only a month and year are given, the last day of the month is presumed. If only a year is given, the last day of the year is presumed.

☛ The signature must be that of a proper party. For an individual, it must agree with the typed name of the applicant. For a partnership, it must be a signature of a general partner. For a corporation, it must be a signature of an officer holding an office established in the articles of incorporation. For example, if the person signing is designated "general manager" or "trademark manager," the application will probably be rejected. (For foreign applicants see chapter 13.)

ATTORNEYS

Attorneys who are filing an application for a client are reminded to add a clause appointing themselves to prosecute the application. This has been done in the typed application, but the same clause can be added to the prepared forms.

FOREIGN
APPLICATION OR
REGISTRATION

Applicants who rely on a foreign application or registration do not need specimens; do not need to give the dates of use; nor the manner of affixing the mark to the goods. Applicants relying on a foreign application must specify their priority date in the heading of their application.

FOREIGN
APPLICANTS

Foreign applicants must have a *domestic representative*. This is a resident of the United States on whom notices of process can be served regarding the application. The domestic representative will also receive official correspondence unless the applicant is also represented by an attorney in the United States. Designation of a domestic representative can be accomplished with Form 14, or the same wording can be added to one of the application forms or to a typed application.

# SENDING IT IN

A completed application consists of the application itself, the drawing, three specimens, and one application fee for each class in which the mark is to be registered. (As this book was going to press the fee was $245, but there are regular calls to raise it.) You should write or call the Patent and Trademark Office to confirm the cost of the fee before filing. If you send the wrong fee it will be sent back, which will delay your filing date. The phone number is (703) 308-4357. The mailing address is:

Assistant Commissioner of Patents and Trademarks
2900 Crystal Drive
Arlington, VA 22202-3513

Your application package should be sent in by certified mail, return receipt requested. If you send in your package by Express Mail and properly fill in the Express Mail number on your application, the date you mail it will be considered your filing date (unless that day is Saturday, Sunday or a Federal holiday in the District of Columbia). The necessary wording is on the application forms in this book. If you type your application, you must use this same wording.

After the application has been sent in, it will be reviewed for errors and published in the *Official Gazette*. These procedures are explained in chapters 10 and 11 of this book.

# WHAT HAPPENS AFTER FILING 10

After your application has been mailed and the receipt returned, one of several things can happen. The least likely is that your trademark will be routinely registered. More likely, you will get a letter or phone call requesting more information or requiring changes in your application.

One thing that may happen is that you may get your whole packet back along with a letter stating that your application is incomplete. The letter contains a checklist of the possible reasons it may be incomplete. This checklist is included below. Review these reasons before you send in your applications to be sure you don't make any of these mistakes:

1. The applicant has not been identified by name.

2. Applicant has not provided an address to which communication can be directed. (How did they return your application?)

3. The drawing requirements have not been met.

4. No drawing has been submitted.

5. The drawing heading is incomplete. A complete heading includes applicant's name, post office address, dates of first use of the mark both anywhere and in commerce, and the goods recited on the application.

6. The goods or services in connection with which the mark is used have not been identified.

7. The requirements for specimens have not been met. (Some of these reasons do not apply to Intent to Use applications.)

8. The materials submitted as specimens are not acceptable because they are merely reproductions of the drawing.

9. No specimen has been submitted.

10. Your attempted use of the mark has been defective in one of the following ways:

    • The date of use in commerce must be specified and must be prior to the filing date, or

    • To use a foreign application for a basis for use, the U.S. application must be filed within six months of filing the foreign application and must state the country of application, or

    • To use a foreign registration for a basis of use, a certification or certified copy of the registration must be submitted.

11. The correct fee was not included.

12. No fee was included.

13. Your check was unsigned.

14. Your check was not drawn on a U. S. bank.

15. The specimens were too bulky.

After the application has been properly filed and accepted, you will get a small receipt indicating the filing. This should come in the self-addressed, stamped envelope that you included with your application.

A second thing that can happen is that you can receive a letter or phone call from the examining attorney at the Patent and Trademark Office regarding some legal or factual problem with the application. Usually the examiner will tell you what the problem is with your application and what needs to be done to correct it. Pay close attention to his or her instructions. Do exactly what he or she requests. Read each paragraph of the letter and be sure to follow it or answer it exactly. You are given the attorney's phone number that you can call to ask questions to determine what would be acceptable.

Normally, you will be given six months to clear up the problems. There is no reason to wait this long. Usually, you can clear the problems up with a letter that should be sent out immediately. If you do address each issue brought up by the examiner, but have not answered them sufficiently, you will usually be given an additional time period to make further corrections. If you fail to answer any issue, then your application will be considered abandoned.

Response to the examiner's letter may be an explanation or submission of additional materials, or it may require an amendment of the application. If an amendment is required it should be typed in the same layout as the typed application in this book (appendix C) but titled "Amendment." It should explain exactly which parts of the application are to be changed in which way.

For example, an amendment might read:

*In response to Office Action of January 29, 1998, please amend the application referred to above as follows:*

*On page 1, line 2, insert the word -plumbing- before the word "books."*

*On page 1, line 9, replace the words "placing on" with the words -gluing labels onto-.*

Note that the communication from the Patent and Trademark Office is referred to as *Office Action,* and that wording that is contained in the original application is put in quotation marks while new wording is surrounded by dashes.

If the problems with your application seem serious, you should consult the *Trademark Manual of Examining Procedure* that is available from the

Superintendent of Documents (see page 26), or possibly at a law school, university or county law library in your area. You may also wish to consult the Rules of Practice in Trademark Cases contained in 37 CFR Ch.1 and the Trademark Act contained in Title 15, Chapter 22, United States Code, both of which should be in your local law library.

If you are not an attorney and are processing your own application, you may want to consider using the services of an attorney to insure completion of your registration if the problems seem to be serious. If your application is rejected a second time, it may be final and an appeal would be much more expensive. If you do decide to consult an attorney, you should be sure to choose one who has experience with trademarks. When making an appointment, you should explain your situation and ask if the attorney would be willing to draft your amendments or take over your case.

Once your application has been accepted as correctly filed, your mark is ready to be published. If you have filed an Intent to Use application, you cannot file an Amendment to Allege Use after your mark has been approved for publication. You must wait until you receive the Notice of Allowance and then file a Statement of Use.

It usually takes several months before you hear from the Patent and Trademark Office. If you wish to check on the status of your application, you can call them at (703) 305-8747.

# Publication and Opposition 11

Once your trademark application has been reviewed by the trademark office's examining attorney and found acceptable, the next step is publication of your mark in the *Official Gazette of the United States Patent and Trademark Office*. This publication comes out each week and lists new trademarks, trademarks renewed, cancelled, etc. A sample page from the *Official Gazette* is shown on page 76. The price for a single copy is about $10 and you will be given instructions on how to order the issue containing your mark. The purpose of the publication is to let the world know of your application and to see if anyone opposes your registration. There are companies that are hired to read the Gazette and inform businesses if someone is attempting to register a mark similar to their own.

## Opposition to Your Mark

Someone opposing your mark has two choices of action. He or she can file a Letter of Protest with the Director of the Trademark Examining Operation, or he or she can file an *opposition*. Handling an opposition is beyond the scope of this book. Anyone against whom an opposition has been filed should consult an attorney or begin some serious research of the *Rules of Practice in Trademark Cases*, §2.101 to §2.148, or a treatise on the subject such as *Trademark Law and Practice* by Edward C. Vandenburgh. However, a brief explanation of the procedures follows:

**LETTER OF PROTEST**

A *letter of protest* would point out some reason your mark should not be registered, such as another registered mark that is confusingly similar or evidence that you are attempting to register a generic mark. In this way, a person hopes to point out a serious enough problem with your application that it will be rejected by the Trademark Office.

**OPPOSITION**

An *opposition* is an action similar to a lawsuit between the parties that is brought before the Trademark Trial and Appeal Board. The proceeding is conducted just like a trial in Federal District Court and is governed by the Federal Rules of Civil Procedure.

**NOTICE OF OPPOSITION**

A *notice of opposition* may come from a large law firm and include a threat of a separate lawsuit for infringement in Federal District Court. In some cases, this may be a serious threat and you may be advised to immediately discontinue use of the mark. This is what the law firms want. But often the letter is just a bluff. Some companies don't want anyone to use any name which in any way resembles their mark. However, they have no right to stop the use of a mark unless it legally infringes theirs. The main issues to consider are whether the marks are indeed similar and confusing, whether the products are similar, whether the parties are dealing in the same channels of commerce, and whether there will be actual confusion. Beginning in 1996, there was a new factor to consider, the Federal Trademark Dilution Act which was discussed in chapter 1.

If there are enough dissimilarities, then you may want to hold out and proceed with the opposition. If you are in your legal rights to register the mark, the person or company that filed the opposition may not want to waste the money involved in a lengthy opposition. As explained below, there are a few things you can do to see if they are serious.

Before making a decision to fight an opposition, you should consult an attorney who specializes in trademark law. His or her expertise can help you decide whether or not you should fight for your mark. Getting an opinion on your case should not be very expensive. However, having a specialist handle your opposition may be more than you can afford, especially if you are a small business. If you do have a good case but cannot afford to have such an expert handle your opposition, you can handle your own case at least long enough to see if they are bluffing, or you might be able to find a local attorney who can help you prepare the proper papers to keep your application alive.

ANSWER

The first step in fighting an opposition is to file an *answer*. An answer in a trademark opposition is similar to one filed in a lawsuit in Federal Court. The original must be filed with the Patent and Trademark Office and a copy sent to the attorney or party filing the opposition. **It must be filed within 30 days or a default will be entered against you and your application cancelled.** The answer is simple to prepare and can give you time to negotiate with the other side or to fight them. It may include specific defenses, for example, if you have been using the mark for many years with the full knowledge of the person opposing you. For more specific instructions, consult one of the treatises contained in the bibliography of this book. They should be available in most law libraries.

THREAT OF LAWSUIT

In addition to the opposition, you may get a letter from the attorney for the other party that threatens a federal lawsuit against you for infringement of their mark. While such a threat should not be taken lightly, it should be kept in mind that this may also be a bluff. Such a lawsuit would most likely be required to be filed in your district. If the other party is located a thousand miles away, it will be quite a burden for him. Even his attorneys will probably not be excited about it because they may have to hire an attorney in your area to prosecute the case.

The best way to respond to such a threat is to send a letter (preferably from an attorney) saying that you have received their letter, that you do not wish to violate their rights, that you are researching the law on the matter, and that upon determining your legal status you will immediately do whatever is necessary to comply with the law. This will show your good faith and give you the opportunity to fight back if they are legally wrong and just bluffing.

INTERROGATORIES

After your answer has been filed (or together with your answer), you can file *interrogatories* on the other side. These are written questions that the opposing party must answer under oath. These will help you get the information you need to decide if they have a good case.

For example, suppose you filed for a trademark of the word "Maple" for a computer software accounting program (in class 9), and suppose a large company that has registered Maple on machine tools (in class 7) files an opposition saying that they use software in their products. To find out if they have a good case, you should send them interrogatories similar to the following:

1. In which of your products do you use computer programs?

2. On what date did you begin using computer programs in each of your products?

3. What function does the computer program serve in each product?

4. Do you sell any of your computer programs separate and apart from the products?

5. During each of the last three years what percentage of your sales were to accountants?

The purpose of your questions should be to generate facts that the opposer's products are in a different field of commerce and that there will be no confusion between your products. In the above example, if one product will be a computer program sold to accountants and the other just the internal part of a tool used by an auto maker, then there is no legal basis for denying your registration.

Interrogatories are a good way to find out how serious a party is in fighting your registration. If your questions require a lot of time to research years of records, they may decide it is not worth the trouble. If they do not take the time to answer your questions or take further action on their opposition, it may be considered abandoned. If they do go through a lot of trouble to provide the answers, they are probably serious about the opposition and you can decide if you want to come to an agreement with them or to give up.

If no opposition has been filed, if it has been filed and then abandoned or if it has been filed and the applicant prevails, then the trademark is issued. A copy of a trademark is shown on pages 77 and 78.

# SAMPLE PAGE FROM THE OFFICIAL GAZETTE

TM 68           OFFICIAL GAZETTE           APRIL 29, 1986

**CLASS 16—(Continued).**

SN 546,693. THOMAS INDUSTRIES INC., LOUISVILLE, KY. FILED 7-8-1985.

## PRO-PERFECT

FOR PAINT BRUSHES AND PAINT ROLLERS FOR USE IN INTERIOR AND EXTERIOR DECORATING AND REPAIR OF DWELLINGS AND OTHER STRUCTURES, AND OF UNITS OR PORTIONS THEREOF (U.S. CL. 29). FIRST USE 6-19-1978; IN COMMERCE 6-19-1978.

---

SN 556,940. 13-30 CORPORATION, KNOXVILLE, TN. FILED 9-5-1985.

## PARENTING ADVISER

NO CLAIM IS MADE TO THE EXCLUSIVE RIGHT TO USE "PARENTING", APART FROM THE MARK AS SHOWN.
FOR POSTERS AND BOOKLETS CONTAINING ITEMS OF INTEREST TO PARENTS (U.S. CL. 38).
FIRST USE 3-14-1985; IN COMMERCE 3-14-1985.

---

SN 559,246. MURRAY, BILL, DBA BAM PRODUCTIONS, SHARON, PA. FILED 9-20-1985.

NO CLAIM IS MADE TO THE EXCLUSIVE RIGHT TO USE "PRODUCTIONS", APART FROM THE MARK AS SHOWN.
FOR COMIC BOOKS (U.S. CL. 38).
FIRST USE 7-1-1985; IN COMMERCE 9-1-1985.

---

SN 559,380. AUTOMOTIVE MANAGEMENT GROUP, INC., SHAWNEE MISSION, KS. FILED 9-20-1985.

## AUTOCOMPUTING REPORT

NO CLAIM IS MADE TO THE EXCLUSIVE RIGHT TO USE "REPORT", APART FROM THE MARK AS SHOWN.
FOR PRINTS AND PUBLICATIONS, NAMELY, A MAGAZINE PROMOTING THE USE OF MICRO AND OTHER COMPUTERS (U.S. CL. 38).
FIRST USE 8-1-1985; IN COMMERCE 8-1-1985.

**CLASS 16—(Continued).**

SN 560,464. HILL, MARSHA A., SILVER SPRING, MD. FILED 9-27-1985.

NO CLAIM IS MADE TO THE EXCLUSIVE RIGHT TO USE "CALENDARS", APART FROM THE MARK AS SHOWN.
THE LINING SHOWN IN THE MARK IS A FEATURE OF THE MARK, AND IS NOT INTENDED TO INDICATE COLOR.
FOR INDIVIDUALIZED, PERSONAL PHOTO CALENDARS (U.S. CLS. 37 AND 38).
FIRST USE 11-0-1984; IN COMMERCE 9-24-1985.

---

SN 562,719. OLMEC CORPORATION, NEW YORK, NY. FILED 10-11-1985.

## RULERS OF THE SUN

FOR PRINTED MATTER, NAMELY, COMIC BOOKS (U.S. CL. 38).
FIRST USE 10-7-1985; IN COMMERCE 10-7-1985.

---

SN 563,434. SPHINX INTERNATIONAL, INC., CLEARWATER, FL. FILED 10-16-1985.

## SPHINX

FOR LAW BOOKS AND LEGAL FORMS (U.S. CLS. 37 AND 38).
FIRST USE 7-20-1983; IN COMMERCE 7-20-1983.

# SAMPLE TRADEMARK

**N⁰ 1402110**

## THE UNITED STATES OF AMERICA

### CERTIFICATE OF REGISTRATION

This is to certify that the records of the Patent and Trademark Office show that an application was filed in said Office for registration of the Mark shown herein, a copy of said Mark and pertinent data from the Application being annexed hereto and made a part hereof,

And there having been due compliance with the requirements of the law and with the regulations prescribed by the Commissioner of Patents and Trademarks,

Upon examination, it appeared that the applicant was entitled to have said Mark registered under the Trademark Act of 1946, and the said Mark has been duly registered this day in the Patent and Trademark Office on the

### PRINCIPAL REGISTER

to the registrant named herein.

This registration shall remain in force for Twenty Years unless sooner terminated as provided by law.

In Testimony Whereof I have hereunto set my hand and caused the seal of the Patent and Trademark Office to be affixed this twenty-second day of July 1986.

*Donald J. Quigg*

**Commissioner of Patents and Trademarks**

(Cover)

Int. Cl.: 16

Prior U.S. Cls.: 37 and 38

**United States Patent and Trademark Office**   Reg. No. 1,402,110
Registered July 22, 1986

**TRADEMARK**
**PRINCIPAL REGISTER**

**SPHINX**

SPHINX INTERNATIONAL, INC. (FLORIDA
  CORPORATION)
806 TURNER ST.
CLEARWATER, FL 33516

FOR: LAW BOOKS AND LEGAL FORMS, IN
CLASS 16 (U.S. CLS. 37 AND 38).

FIRST USE 7-20-1983; IN COMMERCE
7-20-1983.

SER. NO. 563,434, FILED 10-16-1985.

HENRY S. ZAK, EXAMINING ATTORNEY

(Inside)

# PROTECTING YOUR MARK 12

Unlike patents and copyrights that have limited terms, a trademark can last forever. Once your trademark is registered, it will not expire if you continue to use it and follow these rules:

RENEWAL

For marks registered after November 17, 1989, you must renew the mark every ten years. For marks registered prior to that date, the initial term is twenty years. (Form 13 in this book in appendix C can be used to renew a mark.)

SECTION 8 AFFIDAVIT

Your registration will be cancelled at the end of the sixth year unless an affidavit that the mark is still in use has been filed with the Patent and Trademark Office during the preceding 12 month period. This is called a Section 8 Affidavit. (See Form 10 in this book in appendix C.) A specimen showing actual use of your mark must be included with the affidavit.

SECTION 15 AFFIDAVIT

If you file a Section 15 Affidavit stating that the mark has been in continuous use for five years, the mark can be made incontestable for most purposes. (See Form 11 in this book in appendix C.)

COMBINED AFFIDAVIT

If the mark has been in continuous use for five years at the time the Section 8 affidavit is due then a combined Section 8 and Section 15 affidavit can be used. (See Form 12 in this book in appendix C.)

USE THE MARK    You must not abandon the mark. If you fail to use the mark for two years, the law says that you are assumed to have abandoned the mark. This can be rebutted in special cases, such as if you have been involved in trademark litigation or if your company has been closed because of a labor strike.

GENERIC    You must not allow the mark to become *generic*. You might think that you could not be more successful than to have your name become synonymous with the product itself. This could eventually cause the loss of a trademark. "Aspirin" and "cellophane" were once trademarks owned by manufacturers of the products. Now anyone can use these words to describe their products. It is possible that Kleenex, Xerox and Band-Aid will also lose their trademarks someday if they do not protect them. That is why you see ads stressing that it is Kleenex brand tissue.

VIGILANCE    You must protect your mark. If others start using it, you must take action to stop the use. The first step is usually to send a cease and desist letter, demanding that they immediately stop using the mark. You can also demand an accounting of all the money they made using the mark, or use it as a threat if they do not stop using the mark.

In one case, Westinghouse sued some electronics companies for selling reconditioned circuit breakers as new with the counterfeit Westinghouse trademark labels. Westinghouse lost because it had been buying the circuit breakers from the firms for years without complaining about the violation. *In re Circuit Breaker Litig.*, 106 F.3d 894 (7th Cir. 1996).

One thing to be careful about before sending a cease and desist letter is to make sure you have superior rights to the mark. We know of one case where a company sent a letter demanding that another company stop using a similar mark, but the second company had registered their trademark one month before the first company! While the designs of the two marks weren't completely similar, it would be hard for the first company to argue this since they had already claimed in their cease and desist letter that the marks were similar.

LICENSEES

You must control the use of your mark by licensees. If you license someone to use your mark on goods, you must reserve or exercise control over what type and quality of goods on which the mark is used.

RESTRAINT OF TRADE

You must not use the mark in any attempt to restrain trade. For example, there are anti-trust laws that stipulate that the sale of one product cannot be tied to the purchase of another. If you do so with your trademark, you may lose your rights.

DESIGNATION

Whenever you use a word or symbol to identify your goods, until it is registered, you should place the letters "TM" next to it for goods or "SM" for services. This lets the world know that you are claiming it as your mark.

After your mark has been registered (and not before!) you should use one of the following designations next to your mark:

®

Registered in the U.S. Patent and Trademark Office

Reg. U.S. Pat. & Tm. Off.

If you fail to use one of the above, you will lose your right to collect damages from persons who infringe your mark.

CUSTOMS REGISTRATION

If you have reason to believe that someone will be importing counterfeit goods with your trademark on them, you can register your mark with the U. S. Customs Service, Intellectual Property Rights Branch. To do so you need to send them a status copy of your registration along with five copies and a fee of $190 for each class of goods for which your mark is registered. You can use Form 18 in the book.

ASSIGNING YOUR MARK

If you wish to transfer your rights to the trademark to someone else, an Assignment of Trademark form (Form 15 in this book in appendix C) should be filed in the Patent and Trademark Office along with a cover sheet (Form 16 in this book). To find out the current filing fee for an Assignment of Trademark, call (703) 308-4357.

# FOREIGN APPLICANTS 13

For applicants from countries that are members of the Paris Convention or the Pan-American Convention, the process of filing in the United States is simple.

These applicants may rely on a their *foreign application* or *foreign registration* and do not need specimens, nor to give the dates of use, nor the manner of affixing the mark to the goods. Applicants relying on a foreign *application* must specify their priority date in the heading of their application.

The following countries are members of the above-mentioned conventions:

| | |
|---|---|
| Algeria | Brazil |
| Argentina | Bulgaria |
| Aruba | Burkina Faso(OAPI) |
| Australia | Burundi |
| Austria | Cameroon(OAPI) |
| Bahamas | Canada |
| Barbados | Central African Republic(OAPI) |
| Belgium | Chad(OAPI) |
| Benin(African Union Nations) (OAPI) | China (People's Republic) |

Commonwealth of Independent States

Congo(OAPI)

Cook Islands

Cuba

Cyprus

Czech Republic

Denmark

Dominican Republic

Egypt

Finland

France(includes all overseas Departments
    and Territories)

Gabon(OAPI)

Germany

Ghana

Greece

Guinea

Haiti

Hong Kong

Hungary

Iceland

Indonesia

Iran

Iraq

Ireland

Isle of Man

Israel

Italy

Ivory Coast (OAPI)

Japan

Jordan

Kenya

Korea, North

Korea, South

Lebanon

Libya

Liechtenstein

Luxembourg

Malawi

Malaysia

Mali(OAPI)

Malta

Mauritania(OAPI)

Mauritius

Mexico

Monaco

Mongolia

Morocco

Netherlands(Benelux Nations)

New Zealand

Niger(OAPI)

Nigeria

Norway

Philippines

Poland

Portugal

Puerto Rico

Romania

Rwanda

San Marino

Senegal(OAPI)

Slovak Republic

South Africa

Spain

Sri Lanka(formerly Ceylon)

Sudan

Suriname

Sweden

Switzerland

Syria

Tanzania

Togo(OAPI)

Tokelau Islands

Trinidad & Tobago

Tunisia

Turkey

Uganda

United Kingdom

United States (extends to all territories & possessions including Puerto Rico)

Uruguay

Vietnam

Yugoslavia

Zaire

Zambia

Zimbabwe

Applicants from countries that are not members of the above conventions, but who are from countries that are members of the Buenos Aires Convention or countries that offer reciprocal registration rights to U.S. applicants, may apply for registration based upon their foreign registration but not based upon their foreign application. These countries include:

**Buenos Aires Convention:**

Bolivia

Ecuador

**Reciprocal Registration:**

Antigua & Barbados

Belize

Brunei

Dominica

Fiji

Gambia

Grenada

Guyana

India

Jamaica

Kiribati

Lesotho

Pakistan

Saint Kitts and Nevis

Saint Lucia

Saint Vincent and the Grenadines

Seychelles

Sierra Leone

Singapore

Taiwan (Republic of China)

Tonga

Tuvalu

Venezuela

Foreign applicants must have a *domestic representative*. This is a resident of the United States on whom notices or process can be served regarding the application. The domestic representative will also receive official correspondence unless the applicant is also represented by an attorney in the United States. Designation of a domestic representative can be accomplished with Form 14 included in this book, or the same wording can be added to one of the forms or to a typed application.

One common problem with the foreign application is that the person signing does not have the clear authority to do so. More than 400 applications are rejected by the Patent and Trademark Office annually for this reason. Because foreign entities are not always equivalent to U.S. entities, it can be unclear to the trademark examining attorneys whether the person who signed the application had the correct authority.

Under trademark law the correct person to sign is an officer of the legal entity. An officer is defined as a person who holds an office which is established in the articles of incorporation or bylaws. Thus, a person signing as "proxy holder," "trademark manager," or "executive director" will not clearly have the authority to sign.

For some countries, such as Germany, a proper party to sign would be the "director," "manager," or "procurist." In Great Britain, the "registrar" or "confidential clerk" would be proper. To make clear to the examining attorney that the proper party signed the application, it is advisable to add the following statement to the application: "The undersigned is the *[person's title]* of applicant. Under the laws of *[entity's country]*, the position of the person signing is equivalent to that of an officer of a United States corporation."

The following is a list of common types of foreign business entities and the person authorized to sign the trademark application:

GERMANY:

Aktiengesellschaft (A.G.)—manager or director

Gesellschaft mit beschrankter Haftung (G.m.b.H.)—manager

Kommanditgesellschaft (K.G.)—manager

Stiftung—mandatory and deputy mandatory

GREAT BRITAIN:

Public Limited Company(PLC,plc)—chairman of the board of directors, deputy chairman of the board of directors, chief executive director, financial director, secretary

Private Limited Company(Limited, Ltd.)—managing director, director, secretary

Company(not corporation)—the owner of the business

JAPAN:

Kabushiki Kaisha—representative director, director (which may be a president, vice president, executive director, managing director)

Yugen Kaisha—director

Gomei Kaisha—representative partner, business executing partner

Goshi Kaisha—business executing partner

FRANCE:

Societe Anonyme (SA)—president

Societe a Responsabilite Limitee (SARL)—manager

Societe en Commandite par Actions—manager

Other officers who can be authorized to sign documents by special resolutions or statutes of these entitles—financial director, secretary

ITALY:

Societa per azioni—president, vice president, manager, manager of the board of directors

Societa a responsabilita limitata—president, vice president, manager, manager of the board of directors

Societa in nome colletivo—partner

Societa semplive—partner

Societa cooperativa—president, director of the cooperative company

# STATE REGISTRATION 14

In addition to federal registration of trademarks, each state has its own system of registration and protection. If you plan to offer your product or service nationwide, you should proceed immediately with federal registration as described in chapters 6 or 9 of this book. If you do not yet qualify for federal registration or if your business is small and you aren't ready to pay the federal filing fee (presently $245), you can register your mark with your state. The state registration is in most cases much cheaper and simpler than federal registration. In some states the registration fee is as low as $5 or $10.

The main benefit of either state or federal registration is that it is legal notice that you claim some interest in the mark. For federal registration, this notice applies to the entire country; for state registration, it applies only to your state. The benefit of this legal notice is that you can keep others from beginning to use the mark in the future. If someone was already using the mark before you registered it, you cannot stop them from continuing to use it (since they began first), but you can keep them from expanding their use into other areas. People thinking of using your mark will be more likely to find it in their search, and therefore less likely to use it.

A second benefit of state registration is that in some states it offers you certain legal presumptions if you ever have to go to court. For example, without state registration you will have to present evidence to the court that you used the name on a certain date and for certain goods. This may be expensive and time consuming since you would have to provide witnesses and records of your use. State registration (in some states), allows you to present your certificate and these things are presumed.

A more practical benefit is that your registration is a psychological advantage. Two people fighting over their unregistered claims to the mark appear to be on equal footing, but if one is registered, and *has a certificate issued by the state*, the other person will look and feel disadvantaged.

A chart listing the trademark statutes of each state and the types of trademarks available is found on the next three pages..

Each state has its own form, fee schedule and local requirements. To register a name with your state, you should order forms and information directly from your state trademark office. The addresses for these offices are on the following pages.

# STATE TRADEMARK LAWS

| State | Trademark Statute | Fee | Presumptions | Service Marks | Trade Names |
|---|---|---|---|---|---|
| Alabama | §8-12-6 | $30 | No | Yes | Yes |
| Alaska | §45.50.010 | 50 | No | No | No |
| Arizona | §44-1441 | 15 | No | Yes | No |
| Arkansas | §4-71-101 | 50 | No | Yes | No |
| California | CB&PC §14200 | 70 | Yes | Yes | No |
| Colorado | §7-70-102 | 50 | No | Yes | No |
| Connecticut | CGS 621a§35-11a | 50 | Yes | Yes | No |
| Delaware | 6 Del. C. §3301 | 25 | No | Yes | No |
| Florida | §495.011 | 87.50 | Yes | Yes | No |
| Georgia | §10-1-440 | 15 | No | Yes | No |
| Hawaii | §482-2 | 50 | No | Yes | Yes |
| Idaho | §48-501 | 30 | No | Yes | No |
| Illinois | Ch. 140 ¶8-22 | 10 | Yes | Yes | No |
| Indiana | §24-2-1-1 | 10 | No | Yes | No |
| Iowa | Ch. 548 | 10 | Yes | Yes | No |
| Kansas | 81-111 | 25 | No | Yes | No |
| Kentucky | KRS 365.570 | 10 | No | Yes | No |
| Louisiana | T. 9, §§211-224 | 50 | No | Yes | Yes |
| Maine | T. 10, §§1521-1532 | 50 | No | Yes | No |
| Maryland | art. 41, §3-101 | 50 | No | Yes | No |

| State | Trademark Statute | Fee | Presumptions | Service Marks | Trade Names |
|---|---|---|---|---|---|
| Massachusetts | c 110B | 50 | Yes | Yes | No |
| Michigan | MSA §18.638(21) | 50 | Yes | Yes | No |
| Minnesota | 333.20 | 50 | Yes | Yes | No |
| Mississippi | 75-25-3 | 50 | No | Yes | No |
| Missouri | 417.005-.031 | 50 | No | Yes | No |
| Montana | 30-13-301 | 20 | No | Yes | No |
| Nebraska | 87-210 | 100 | No | Yes | No |
| Nevada | 600.340-.456 | 50 | Yes | Yes | No |
| New Hampshire | c 350-A | 50 | No | Yes | No |
| New Jersey | T.t 56 c3§§13.1-13.9 | 50 | No | Yes | No |
| New Mexico | 57-3 | 25 | No | Yes | Yes |
| New York | T.t.K of Arts & Cult. | 50 | No | Yes | No |
| North Carolina | 80-2 to 80-15 | 50 | No | Yes | No |
| North Dakota | 47-22-02 | 30 | No | No | No |
| Ohio | 1329.54 | 20 | No | Yes | No |
| Oklahoma | 78-21 et seq. | 50 | No | Yes | No |
| Oregon | 647.029, 035 | 20 | Yes | Yes | No |
| Pennsylvania | 54*1102, 1111 | 52 | No | Yes | No |
| Puerto Rico | 10-191, et seq. | 100 | Yes | Yes | Yes |
| Rhode Island | 6-2-1 through 15 | 50 | Yes | Yes | No |
| South Carolina | 39-15-10 to -750 | 15 | No | Yes | No |
| South Dakota | 37-6 | 10 | Yes | Yes | No |

| State | Trademark Statute | Fee | Presumptions | Service Marks | Trade Names |
|-------|-------------------|-----|--------------|---------------|-------------|
| Tennessee | 47-25-502 | 5 | No | Yes | No |
| Texas | Cus. & com. 16.01 et seq. | 50 | Yes | Yes | No |
| Utah | Title 70 c. 3 | 20 | Yes | Yes | No |
| Vermont | 9-2521-75 | 10 | No | No | No |
| Virginia | 59.1-81 | 30 | No | Yes | No |
| Washington | 19.77 | 50 | Yes | Yes | No |
| West Virginia | c 47, art. 2 §§1.2 | 10 | Yes | No | No |
| Wisconsin | 132.01 | 15 | Yes | No | No |
| Wyoming | 40-1-101 | 100 | No | Yes | Yes |

# STATE TRADEMARK OFFICES

**Alabama**
Trademark Division
Secretary of State
State Office Building, Room 528
Montgomery, AL 36130
(205) 242-5325
http://www.alalinc.net/alsecst/corporat.htm

**Alaska**
Corporations Section
Dept. of Commerce & Econ. Dev.
P. O. Box D
Juneau, AK 99811
(907) 465-2530
http://www.commerce.state.ak.us/dced/bsc/corps.htm

**Arizona**
Trademark Division
Secretary of State
1700 W. Washington St.
Phoenix, AZ 85007
(602) 542-6187
http://www.cc.state.az.us/

**Arkansas**
Trademark Division
Secretary of State
State Capitol
Little Rock, AR 72201-1094
(501) 682-3481
http://www.state.ar.us/sos/index.html

**California**
Trademark Unit
Secretary of State
1230 "J" Street
Sacramento, CA 95814
(916) 445-9872
http://www.ss.ca.gov/

**Colorado**
Corporations Office
Secretary of State
1560 Broadway, #200
Denver, CO 80202
(303) 894-2251
http://www.state.co.us/gov_dir/sos/manual.html

**Connecticut**
Trademarks Division
Secretary of State
30 Trinity Street
Hartford, CT 06106
(860) 509-6003
http://www.state.ct.us/sots/

**Delaware**
Trademark Filings
Division of Corporations
P. O. Box 898
Dover, DE 19903
(302) 739-3073
http://www.state.de.us/govern/agencies/corp/corp.htm

**Florida**
Trademark Section
Division of Corporations
P. O. Box 6327
Tallahassee, FL 32301
(904) 487-6051
http://www.dos.state.fla.us

**Georgia**
Secretary of State
306 W. Floyd Towers
2 MLK Drive
Atlanta, GA 30334
(404) 656-2861
http://www.SOS.State.Ga.US/

**Hawaii**
Business Registration Division
Dept. of Commerce & Consumer Affairs
1010 Richards St.
Honolulu, HI 96813
(808) 586-2730
http://www.SOS.State.Ga.US/

**Idaho**
Trademark Division
Secretary of State
Statehouse Room 203
Boise, ID 83720
(208) 334-2300
http://www.idsos.state.id.us/

**Illinois**
Trademark Division
Secretary of State
111 East Monroe
Springfield, IL 62756
(217) 782-7017
http://www.sos.state.il.us/depts/bus_serv/bus_home.html

**Indiana**
Trademark Division
Secretary of State
State House Room 155
Indianapolis, IN 46204
(317) 232-6540
[not yet operational]

**Iowa**
Corporate Division
Secretary of State
Hoover Bldg.
Des Moines, IA 50319
(515) 281-5204
http://www.sos.state.ia.us/

**Kansas**
Trademark Division
Secretary of State
Statehouse Bldg., Room 235N
Topeka, KS 66612
(913) 296-2034
http://www.state.ks.us/public/sos/

**Kentucky**
Trademark Division
Secretary of State
Frankfort, KY 40601
(502) 564-2848
http://www.sos.state.ky.us/

**Louisiana**
Corporation Division
Secretary of State
P. O. Box 94125
Baton Rouge, LA 70804-9125
(504) 925-4704
http://www.sec.state.la.us/

**Maine**
Division of Public Administration
Department of State
State House Station 101
Augusta, ME 04333
(207) 289-4195
http://www.state.me.us/sos/sos.htm

**Maryland**
Trademark Division
Secretary of State
State House
Annapolis, MD 21404
(301) 974-5521
http://www.dat.state.md.us/charter.html

**Massachusetts**
Trademark Division
Secretary of State
One Ashburton Place #1711
Boston, MA 02108
(617) 727-8329
http://www.state.ma.us/massgov.htm

**Michigan**
Corporation Division
Department of Commerce
P. O. Box 30054
Lansing, MI 48909
(517) 334-6302
http://www.sos.state.mi.us/

**Minnesota**
Corporation Division
Secretary of State
180 State Office Bldg.
St. Paul, MN 55155
(612) 296-3266
http://www.sos.state.mn.us/bus.html

**Mississippi**
Trademark Division
Secretary of State
P. O. Box 1350
Jackson, MS 32915
(601) 359-1350
http://www.sos.state.ms.us/

**Missouri**
Trademark Division
Secretary of State
P. O. Box 778
Jefferson City, MO 65101
(314) 751-4756
http://mosl.sos.state.mo.us/bus-ser/soscor.html

**Montana**
Trademark Division
Secretary of State
State Capitol
Helena, MT 59620
(406) 444-3665
http://www.mt.gov/sos/biz.htm

**Nebraska**
Trademark Division
Secretary of State
State Capitol Bldg.
Lincoln, NE 68509
(402) 471-4079
http://www.nol.org/home/SOS/services.htm

**Nevada**
Trademark Division
Secretary of State
Capitol Complex
Carson City, NV 89710
(702) 687-5203
http://jvm.com/sos/

**New Hampshire**
Corporation Division
Secretary of State
State House Annex
Concord, NH 03301
(603) 271-3244
[not yet operational]

**New Jersey**
Secretary of State
State House
West State St. CN-300
Trenton, NJ 08625
(609) 984-1900
http://www.state.nj.us/state/

**New Mexico**
Trademark Division
Secretary of State
Capitol Bldg. Rm. 400
Santa Fe, NM 87503
(505) 827-3600
http://www.sos.state.nm.us/

**New York**
Miscellaneous Records
Secretary of State
162 Washington Ave.
Albany, NY 12231
(518) 473-2492
http://www.dos.state.ny.us/

**North Carolina**
Trademark Division
Secretary of State
300 N. Salisbury St.
Raleigh, NC 27611
(919) 733-4161
http://www.secstate.state.nc.us/secstate/

**North Dakota**
Trademark Division
Secretary of State
State Capitol
Bismark, ND 58505
(701) 328-4284
[not yet operational]

**Ohio**
Corporations Department
Secretary of State
30 E. Broad St., 14th Fl.
Columbus, OH 43215
(614) 466-3910
http://www.state.oh.us/sos/

**Oklahoma**
Trademark Division
Secretary of State
101 State Capitol Bldg.
Oklahoma City, OK 73105
(405) 521-3911
http://www.occ.state.ok.us/

**Oregon**
Director, Corporation Division
Secretary of State
158 - 12th Street NE
Salem, OR 97310-0210
(503) 986-2200
http://www.sos.state.or.us/

**Pennsylvania**
Corporation Bureau
Secretary of State
308 North Office Bldg.
Harrisburg, PA 17120
(717) 787-1057
http://www.state.pa.us/PA_Exec/State/

**Puerto Rico**
Trademark Division
Secretary of State
P. O. Box 3271
San Juan, PR 00904
(809) 722-2121 Ext. 337
[not yet operational]

**Rhode Island**
Trademark Division
Secretary of State
100 No. Main St
Providence, RI 02903
(401) 277-2340
http://www.state.ri.us/STDEPT/sdlink.htm

**South Carolina**
Trademark Division
Secretary of State
P. O. Box 11350
Columbia, SC 29211
(803) 734-2158
http://www.leginfo.state.sc.us/secretary.html

**South Dakota**
Secretary of State
State Capitol Bldg.
500 East Capitol
Pierre, SD 57501
(605) 773-3537
http://www.state.sd.us/state/executive/sos/sos.htm

**Tennessee**
Trademark Division
Secretary of State
James K. Polk Bldg. #500
Nashville, TN 37219
(615) 741-0531
http://www.state.tn.us/sos/index.htm

**Texas**
Trademark Division
Secretary of State
Box 13697, Capitol Sta.
Austin, TX 78711-3697
(512) 463-5576
http://www.state.tx.us/agency/307.html

**Utah**
Div. of Corporations
Heber M. Wells Bldg.
160 E. 300 South St.
Salt Lake City, UT 84111
(801) 530-4849
http://www.commerce.state.ut.us/web/commerce/
corporat/corpcoc.htm

**Vermont**
Corporations Division
Secretary of State
State Office Building
Montpelier, VT 05602
(802) 828-2386
http://www.sec.state.vt.us/

**Virginia**
Div. of Securities & Retail Franchises
State Corp. Commission
1220 Bank Street
Richmond, VA 84111
(804) 271-9051
http://www.state.va.us/scc/index.html

**Washington**
Corporations Division
Secretary of State
505 E. Union St., 2nd Fl.
Olympia, WA 98504
(206) 753-7120
http://www.wa.gov/sec/

**West Virginia**
Corporations Division
Secretary of State
State Capitol
Charleston, WV 25305
(304) 558-8000
[not yet operational]

**Wisconsin**
Trademark Division
Secretary of State
P. O. Box 7848
Madison, WI 53707
(608) 266-5653
[not yet operational]

**Wyoming**
Corporation Division
Secretary of State
Capitol Bldg.
Cheyenne, WY 82002
(307) 777-7311
http://soswy.state.wy.us/

# OTHER
# PROTECTIONS 15

Although registering a mark is the best way to protect it, an unregistered mark is not without protection. If you are using a mark to distinguish your goods or services, the law protects you from others who would copy them or pass off their goods as yours. There are both federal and state laws that offer protection for marks that are unregistered:

The Lanham Act, which is the federal trademark statute, provides protection for unregistered products from "unfair trade practices." This is contained in section 43(a) of the act. The necessary elements of a violation of the law are as follows:

☞ One party created his product through extensive time, labor, skill or money.

☞ A second party used some aspects of the first party's product in competition with him, gaining an advantage because it was done without the cost.

☞ The second party caused commercial damage to the first.

Where these three factors are true, the first party could win damages against the second in a federal lawsuit. (Also, in some state courts, as explained below.)

However, it should be pointed out that there are many different federal courts in this country, and the rulings are not always consistent. What is illegal in one district may not be illegal in another. Sometimes two federal courts in the same state rule differently on the same issue. This may be because the lawyers didn't present the issues properly, because the judges didn't understand this obscure area of the law or because they just interpreted the law differently.

In some ways, this protection is even stronger than trademark protection since the latter only covers you in one class of goods. Under unfair trade law, if a business has built up a reputation with its name or other aspect of its product, then it can stop anyone from "diluting" the value of its name or reputation.

An example of this protection is the Toys 'R' Us company. Whenever someone tries to use a similar name, such as "Insurance 'R' Us," Toys 'R' Us threatens a federal lawsuit. While insurance is in no way related to toys, and no rational person would mistake the two, the toy company claims that such use dilutes the value of their name and is usually able to intimidate small companies into giving up.

STATE
PROTECTION
Federal trademark protection only covers goods or services that travel across state lines or to a foreign country. In some states, there are statutes similar to the Lanham Act that give state remedies for similar activities. In addition, states without specific statutes have court decisions, or common law, which protects businesses from unfair competition.

Some states have laws that prohibit use of a mark even if there is no customer confusion. These are *dilution* laws. The idea is that if someone uses your mark without your permission, he dilutes the value of your mark. However, dilution laws apply only to marks that are very well known.

If you think someone is violating your rights or you are afraid of violating someone else's, you should research your own state's laws further. On the following pages is a list of which states protect marks against dilution and unfair trade practices.

|  | Dilution Law | Unfair Competition Law |
| --- | --- | --- |
| Alabama | §8-12-17 | No |
| Alaska | §45.50.180 | No |
| Arizona | No | No |
| Arkansas | §4-71-113 | No |
| California | B&PC §14300 | B&PC §17200 |
| Colorado | No | No |
| Connecticut | 621a, §35-11i | No |
| Delaware | 6 Del.C. §3313 | 6 Del.C. §2531 |
| District of Columbia | No | No |
| Florida | §495.151 | §501.201 et seq |
| Georgia | 10-1-451(b) | 23-2-55 |
| Hawaii | No | 480-2; 487-5(5) |
| Idaho | 48-512 | No |
| Illinois | 140, ¶22 | No |
| Indiana | No | No |
| Iowa | 548.11(2) | No |
| Kansas | No | No |
| Kentucky | No | No |
| Louisiana | 51:223.1 | 51:1401 et seq |
| Maine | 10 MRSA §1530 | No |
| Maryland | No | §13-301 |
| Massachusetts | CH. 110B, §12 | No |
| Michigan | No | No |

| | Dilution Law | Unfair Competition Law |
|---|---|---|
| Minnesota | §325D | No |
| Mississippi | §75-25-25 | No |
| Missouri | §417.061(1) | No |
| Montana | §30-13-334 | No |
| Nebraska | §59-1601 | No |
| Nevada | No | No |
| New Hampshire | §350-A:12 | §358-A:2 |
| New Jersey | 13PL1995 c.171 | §56:4-1 |
| New Mexico | 57-3-10 | No |
| New York | G.B.L. §368-d | No |
| North Carolina | No | No |
| North Dakota | No | No |
| Ohio | No | No |
| Oklahoma | No | No |
| Oregon | §647.107 | §646.608(1)(b) |
| Pennsylvania | 54PCSA §1124 | No |
| Rhode Island | §6-2-12 | No |
| South Carolina | §39-15-1105(2) | No |
| South Dakota | No | §37-6-2 |
| Tennessee | §47-25-512 | No |
| Texas | B&CC 16.29 | PC §32.42 |
| Utah | No | No |

| | Dilution Law | Unfair Competition Law |
|---|---|---|
| Vermont | No | 9 VSA §2532 |
| Virginia | No | §18.2-499 |
| Washington | RCW 19.77 | No |
| West Virginia | §47-2-13 | §47-11A-1 et seq |
| Wisconsin | No | No |
| Wyoming | No | No |

# CHECKLISTS 16

# PRESENT USE CHECKLIST

Choose the mark—

✓ Does it project a positive image?

✓ Will it have continued value?

✓ Will it be useful in other states and countries?

✓ Make sure it is not merely descriptive

✓ Make sure it is not forbidden

Search the mark—

✓ Preliminary search of locally available sources

✓ Search Patent and Trademark Office

✓ Common Law search (phone books, directories, etc.)

Use the mark—

✓ Use it *in commerce*

✓ Use must be bona fide

Prepare the application—

✓ Choose right form–trademark/collective/membership/certification

✓ Create drawing

✓ Obtain specimens of mark as actually used

Send it all in—

✓ Application–signed

✓ Drawing

✓ Specimens

✓ Fee

✓ Self-addressed stamped envelope

Answer correspondence—

✓ Follow all instructions to the letter

✓ If opposition–fight it or abandon it

After mark is issued—

✓ File §8 affidavit after fifth anniversary and before sixth anniversary

✓ If use has been continuous, file §8 & §15 affidavit instead

✓ Use ® symbol with your mark

✓ Do not abandon your mark

✓ Do not allow it to become generic

✓ Do not allow others to infringe your mark

✓ Control the use of your mark by licensees

✓ Do not use your mark in restraint of trade

✓ Renew mark every ten years

# INTENT TO USE CHECKLIST

Choose the mark—
       ✓ Does it project a positive image?
       ✓ Will it have continued value?
       ✓ Will it be useful in other states and countries?
       ✓ Make sure it is not merely descriptive
       ✓ Make sure it is not forbidden

Search the mark—
       ✓ Preliminary search of locally available sources
       ✓ Search Patent and Trademark Office
       ✓ Common Law search (phone books, directories, etc.)

Prepare the application—
       ✓ Choose right form–trademark/collective/membership/certification
       ✓ Create drawing

Send it in—
       ✓ Application–signed
       ✓ Drawing
       ✓ Fee
       ✓ Self-addressed stamped envelope

Use the mark—
       ✓ Use it *in commerce*
       ✓ Use must be bona fide

Submit proof of use—
       ✓ Amendment to Allege Use, or Statement of Use
       ✓ Include specimens of use
       ✓ Fee

Answer correspondence—
       ✓ Follow all instructions to the letter
       ✓ If opposition–fight it or abandon it

After mark is issued—
       ✓ File §8 affidavit after fifth anniversary and before sixth anniversary
       ✓ If use has been continuous, file §8 & §15 affidavit instead
       ✓ Use ® with your mark
       ✓ Do not abandon your mark
       ✓ Do not allow it to become generic
       ✓ Do not allow others to infringe your mark
       ✓ Control the use of your mark by licensees
       ✓ Do not use your mark in restraint of trade
       ✓ Renew mark every ten years

# APPENDIX A
# TRADEMARK CLASSIFICATIONS

Before searching your mark you will need to determine which classification the goods or services will fall into. On the following pages are both the International and prior U.S. classification.

If your goods or services clearly fall into one classification you can write it on your application. However if you are not sure, leave it blank and the Patent and Trademark Office will fill it in for you.

# INTERNATIONAL CLASSIFICATIONS

## —Goods—

1. Chemicals used in industry, science, photography, as well as in agriculture, horticulture, and forestry; unprocessed artificial resins; unprocessed plastics; manures; fire extinguishing compositions; tempering and soldering preparations; chemical substances for preserving foodstuffs; tanning substances; adhesives used in industry.

2. Paints, varnishes, lacquers; preservatives against rust and against deterioration of wood; colourants; mordants; raw natural resins; metals in foil and powder form for painters, decorators, printers and artists.

3. Bleaching preparations and other substances for laundry use; cleaning, polishing, scouring and abrasive preparations; soaps; perfumery, essential oils, cosmetics, hair lotions; dentifrices.

4. Industrial oils and greases; lubricants; dust absorbing, wetting and binding compositions; fuel (including motor spirit) and illuminants; candles, wicks.

5. Pharmaceutical, veterinary, and sanitary preparations; dietetic substances adapted for medical use, food for babies; plasters, materials for dressings, material for stopping teeth, dental wax, disinfectants; preparations for destroying vermin; fungicides, herbicides.

6. Common metals and their alloys; metal building materials; transportable buildings of metal; materials of metal for railway racks; non-electric cables and wires of common metal; iron-mongery, small items of metal hardware; pipes and tubes of metal; safes; goods of common metal not included in other classes; ores.

7. Machines and machine tools; motors (except for land vehicles); machine coupling and belting (except for land vehicles); agricultural implements; incubators for eggs.

8. Hand tools and implements (hand-operated); cutlery; side arms; razors.

9. Scientific, nautical, surveying, electric, photographic, cinematographic, optical, weighing, measuring, signalling, checking (supervision), life-saving and teaching apparatus and instruments; apparatus for recording transmission or reproduction of sound or images; magnetic data carriers, recording discs; automatic vending machines and mechanisms for coin-operated apparatus; cash registers, calculating

machines, data processing equipment and computers; fire-extinguishing apparatus.

10. Surgical, medical, dental, and veterinary apparatus and instruments, artificial limbs, eyes and teeth; orthopedic articles; suture materials.

11. Apparatus for lighting, heating, steam generating, cooking, refrigerating, drying, ventilating, water supply, and sanitary purposes.

12. Vehicles; apparatus for locomotion by land, air or water.

13. Firearms; ammunition and projectiles; explosives; fireworks.

14. Precious metals and their alloys and goods in precious metals or coated therewith, not included in other classes; jewelry, precious stones; horological and other chronometric instruments.

15. Musical instruments.

16. Paper and cardboard and goods made from these materials, not included in other classes; printed matter; bookbinding material; photographs; stationery; adhesives for stationery or household purposes; artists' materials; paint brushes; typewriters and office requisites (except furniture); instructional and teaching material (except apparatus); plastic materials for packaging (not included on other classes); playing cards; printers' type; printing blocks.

17. Rubber, gutta-percha, gum, asbestos, mica and goods made from these materials and not included in other classes; plastics in extruded form for use in manufacture; packing, stopping and insulating materials; flexible pipes, not of metal.

18. Leather and imitations of leather, and goods made from these materials and not included in other classes; animal skins, hides; trunks and travelling bags; umbrellas, parasols and walking sticks; whips, harness and saddlery.

19. Building materials (non-metallic); nonmetallic rigid pipes for building; asphalt, pitch and bitumen; non-metallic transportable buildings; monuments, not of metal.

20. Furniture, mirrors, picture frames, goods (not included in other classes) of wood, cork, reed cane, wicker, horn, bone, ivory, whalebone, shell, amber, mother-of-pearl, meerschaum and substitutes for all these materials, or of plastics.

21. Household or kitchen utensils and containers (not of precious metal or coated therewith); combs and sponges;

brushes (except paint brushes); brush-making materials; articles for cleaning purposes; steel wool; unworked or semi-worked glass (except glass used in building); glassware, porcelain and earthenware, not included in other classes.

22. Ropes, string, nets, tents, awnings, tarpaulins, sails, sacks; and bags (not included in other classes); padding and stuffing materials (except of rubber or plastics); raw fibrous textile materials.

23. Yarns and threads, for textile use.

24. Textile and textile goods, not included in other classes; bed and table covers.

25. Clothing, footwear, headgear.

26. Lace and embroidery, ribbons and braid; buttons, hooks and eyes, pins and needles; artificial flowers.

27. Carpets, rugs, mats and matting; linoleum and other materials for covering existing floors; wall hangings (non-textile).

28. Games and playthings; gymnastic and sporting articles not included in other classes; decorations for Christmas trees.

29. Meats, fish, poultry and game; meat extracts; preserved, dried and cooked fruits and vegetables; jellies, jams; eggs, milk and milk products; edible oils and fats; salad dressings; preserves.

30. Coffee, tea, cocoa, sugar, rice, tapioca, sago, artificial coffee; flour, and preparations made from cereals, bread, pastry and confectionery, ices; honey, treacle; yeast, baking-powder; salt, mustard, vinegar, sauces, (except salad dressings) spices; ice.

31. Agricultural, horticultural and forestry products and grains not included in other classes; living animals; fresh fruits and vegetables; seeds, natural pants and flowers; foodstuffs for animals, malt.

32. Beers; mineral and aerated waters and other non-alcoholic drinks; fruit drinks and fruit juices; syrups and other preparations for making beverages.

33. Alcoholic beverages (except beers).

34. Tobacco; smokers' articles; matches.

—Services—

35. Advertising and business.

36. Insurance and financial.

37. Construction and repair.

38. Communication.

39. Transportation and storage.

40. Material treatment.

41. Education and entertainment.

42. Miscellaneous.Prior U.S. Classifications

# PRIOR U.S. CLASSIFICATIONS

## —Goods—

1. Raw or partly prepared materials.

2. Receptacles.

3. Baggage, animal equipments, portfolios, and pocket books.

4. Abrasives and polishing materials.

5. Adhesives.

6. Chemicals and chemical compositions.

7. Cordage.

8. Smokers' articles, not including tobacco products.

9. Explosives, firearms, equipments, and projectiles.

10. Fertilizers.

11. Inks and inking materials.

12. Construction materials.

13. Hardware and plumbing and steamfitting supplies.

14. Metals and metal castings and forgings.

15. Oils and greases.

16. Protective and decorative coatings.

17. Tobacco products.

18. Medicines and pharmaceutical preparations.

19. Vehicles.

20. Linoleum and oiled cloth.

21. Electrical apparatus, machines, and supplies.

22. Games, toys, and sporting goods.

23. Cutlery, machinery, and tools, and parts thereof.

24. Laundry appliances and machines.

25. Locks and safes.

26. Measuring and scientific appliances.

27. Horological instruments.

28. Jewelry and precious-metal ware.

29. Brooms, brushes, and dusters.

30. Crockery, earthenware, and porcelain.

31. Filters and refrigerators.

32. Furniture and upholstery.

33. Glassware.

34. Heating, lighting, and ventilating apparatus.

35. Belting, hose, machinery packing, and nonmetallic tires.

36. Musical instruments and supplies.

37. Paper and stationery.

38. Prints and publications.

39. Clothing.

40. Fancy goods, furnishings, and notions.

41. Canes, parasols, and umbrellas.

42. Knitted, netted, and textile fabrics, and substitutes therefor.

43. Thread and yarn.

44. Dental, medical, and surgical appliances.

45. Soft drinks and carbonated waters.

46. Foods and ingredients of foods.

47. Wines.

48. Malt beverages and liquors.

50. Merchandise not otherwise classified.

51. Cosmetics and toilet preparations.

52. Detergents and soaps.

## —Services—

100. Miscellaneous.

101. Advertising and business.

102. Insurance and financial

103. Construction and repair.

104. Communication.

105. Transportation and storage.

106. Material treatment.

107. Education and entertainment.

# APPENDIX B
# SAMPLE FILLED-IN FORMS

The following pages contain the forms mentioned throughout this book. They may be either removed from this book and used, or photocopied.

ADOLPH BUSH
_____
[Your Name]
123 MALT LANE
_____
[Address]
EAST ST. LOUIS, IL 61201
_____
[City, State Zip]
217-555-1212
_____
[Phone]


January 5, 2000
[Date]


Hon Commissioner of Patents and Trademarks
Washington, DC 20231

Re: In Use Trademark Application


Sir:


Enclosed for filing please find trademark application papers of
_____BUSH BROTHERS_____ for the mark
"_____OLD NAG_____" in International Class _32___ (Prior
U.S. Class _48___ ) together with the drawing, three specimens and
the filing fee of $245.

A self-addressed, stamped envelope is enclosed for return of the
receipt.


Respectfully submitted,



*Adolph Bush*
_____
[Your Name]

AMALGAMATED DANCERS' UNION, LOCAL 55, INC.
[Your Name]
257 83RD ST.
[Address]
NEW YORK, NY 10011
[City, State Zip]
(212)555-0000
[Phone]


February 10, 1999
[Date]


Hon Commissioner of Patents and Trademarks
Washington, DC 20231

Re: Intent-to-Use Trademark Application


Sir:


Enclosed for filing please find trademark application papers of
AMALGAMATED DANCERS' UNION, LOCAL 55, INC. for the mark
"        ADU - LOCAL 55        " in International Class      200 (Prior
U.S. Class        ) together with the drawing and the filing fee of
$245.

A self-addressed, stamped envelope is enclosed for return of the
receipt.


Respectfully submitted,


*John Doe*

[Your Name]

| TRADEMARK/SERVICE MARK APPLICATION, PRINCIPAL REGISTER, WITH DECLARATION | MARK (Word(s) and/or Design)<br><br>OLD NAG | CLASS NO.<br>(If known)<br><br>32 |
|---|---|---|

## TO THE ASSISTANT COMMISSIONER FOR TRADEMARKS:

**APPLICANT'S NAME:** BUSH BROTHERS

**APPLICANT'S MAILING ADDRESS:**

(Display address exactly as it should appear on registration)

123 MALT LANE
EAST ST. LOUIS, IL 61201

### APPLICANT'S ENTITY TYPE: (Check one and supply requested information)

| | |
|---|---|
| | Individual - Citizen of (Country): |
| X | Partnership - State where organized (Country, if appropriate): ILLINOIS<br>Names and Citizenship (Country) of General Partners:<br>ADOLPH BUSH<br>MARVIN BUSH |
| | Corporation - State (Country, if appropriate) of Incorporation: |
| | Other (Specify Nature of Entity and Domicile): |

### GOODS AND/OR SERVICES:

Applicant requests registration of the trademark/service mark shown in the accompanying drawing in the United States Patent and Trademark Office on the Principal Register established by the Act of July 5, 1946 (15 U.S.C. 1051 et. seq., as amended) for the following goods/services **(SPECIFIC GOODS AND/OR SERVICES MUST BE INSERTED HERE)**

BEER AND MALT LIQUOR

### BASIS FOR APPLICATION: (Check boxes which apply, but never both the first AND second boxes, and supply requested information related to each box checked.)

| | |
|---|---|
| [X] | Applicant is using the mark in commerce on or in connection with the above identified goods/services. (15 U.S.C. 1051(a), as amended.) Three specimens showing the mark as used in commerce are submitted with this application.<br>• Date of first use of the mark in commerce which the U.S. Congress may regulate (for example, interstate or between the U.S. and a foreign country): JULY 5, 1999<br>• Specify the type of commerce: INTERSTATE<br>(for example, interstate or between the U.S. and a specified foreign country)<br>• Date of first use anywhere (the same as or before use in commerce date): MAY 6, 1966<br>• Specify intended manner or mode of use of mark on or in connection with the goods/services: TRADEMARK IS PAINTED ON CONTAINERS IN WHICH THE PRODUCT IS SHIPPED<br>(for example, trademark is applied to labels, service mark is used in advertisements) |
| [ ] | Applicant has a bona fide intention to use the mark in commerce on or in connection with the above identified goods/services. (15 U.S.C. 1051(b), as amended.)<br>• Specify manner or mode of use of mark on or in connection with the goods/services:<br>(for example, trademark will be applied to labels, service mark will be used in advertisements) |
| [ ] | Applicant has a bona fide intention to use the mark in commerce on or in connection with the above identified goods/services, and asserts a claim of priority based upon a foreign application in accordance with 15 U.S.C. 1126(d), as amended.<br>• Country of foreign filing:_____ • Date of foreign filing:_____ |
| [ ] | Applicant has a bona fide intention to use the mark in commerce on or in connection with the above identified goods/services and, accompanying this application, submits a certification or certified copy of a foreign registration in accordance with 15 U.S.C 1126(e), as amended.<br>• Country of registration:_____ • Registration number:_____ |

**NOTE: Declaration, on Reverse Side, MUST be Signed**

*form 4*

| COLLECTIVE TRADEMARK/SERVICE MARK APPLICATION, PRINCIPAL REGISTER, WITH DECLARATION | MARK (Word(s) and/or Design)  U.S.U.S. | CLASS NO. (If known)  18 |

## TO THE ASSISTANT COMMISSIONER FOR TRADEMARKS:

**APPLICANT'S NAME:** UNITED STATES UMBRELLA SOCIETY, INC.

**APPLICANT'S MAILING ADDRESS:** 101 WARF STREET

(Display address exactly as it should appear on registration) SEATTLE, WA 97654

### APPLICANT'S ENTITY TYPE: (Check one and supply requested information)

| | Individual - Citizen of (Country): |
| | Partnership - State where organized (Country, if appropriate): _____ Names and Citizenship (Country) of General Partners: _____ |
| X | Corporation - State (Country, if appropriate) of Incorporation: WASHINGTON |
| | Other (Specific Nature of Entity and Domicile): |

### GOODS AND/OR SERVICES:

Applicant requests registration of the collective mark shown in the accompanying drawing in the United States Patent and Trademark Office on the Principal Register established by the Act of July 5, 1946 (15 U.S.C. 1051 et. seq., as amended) for the following goods/services **(SPECIFIC GOODS AND/OR SERVICES MUST BE INSERTED HERE)**: _____

UMBRELLAS

### BASIS FOR APPLICATION: (Check boxes which apply, but never both the first AND second boxes, and supply requested information related to each box checked.)

| [ ] | Applicant is exercising legitimate control over the use of the mark in commerce by its members on or in connection with the above identified goods/services. (15 U.S.C. 1051 (a) and 1054, as amended.) Three specimens showing the mark as used by the members in commerce are submitted with this application.  • Date of first use of the mark in commerce which the U.S. Congress may regulate (for example, interstate or between the U.S. and a foreign country): _____  • Specify the type of commerce: _____  (for example, interstate or between the U.S. and a specified foreign country)  • Date of first use anywhere (the same as or before use in commerce date): _____  • Specify intended manner or mode of use of mark on or in connection with the goods/services: _____  (for example, trademark is applied to labels, service mark is used in advertisements) |
| [ ] | Applicant has a bona fide intention to exercise legitimate control over the use of the mark in commerce by its members on or in connection with the above-identified good/services. (15 U.S. C. 1051(b) and 1054, as amended.)  • Specify intended manner or mode of use of mark on or in connection with the goods/services: _____  (for example, trademark will be applied to labels, service mark will be used in advertisements) |
| [x] | Applicant has a bona fide intention to exercise legitimate control over the use of the mark in commerce by its members on or in connection with the above identified goods/services, and asserts a claim of priority based upon a foreign application in accordance with 15 U.S.C. 1126(d), as amended.  • Country of foreign filing: GREAT BRITAIN          • Date of foreign filing: AUGUST 9, 1999 |
| [ ] | Applicant has a bona fide intention to exercise legitimate control over the use of the mark in commerce by its members on or in connection with the above identified goods/services and, accompanying this application, submits a certification or certified copy of a foreign registration in accordance with 15 U.S.C 1126(e), as amended.  • Country of registration: _____          • Registration number: _____ |

### NOTE: Declaration, on Reverse Side, MUST be Signed

PTO Form 1478(a) (REV 6/96)
OMB No. 0651-0009 (Exp. 06/30/98) There is no requirement to respond to this collection of information unless a currently valid OMB Number is displayed.

U.S. DEPARTMENT OF COMMERCE/Patent and Trademark Office

| COLLECTIVE MEMBERSHIP MARK APPLICATION, PRINCIPAL REGISTER, WITH DECLARATION | MARK (Word(s) and/or Design)  ADU – LOCAL 55 | CLASS NO. 200 |
|---|---|---|

## TO THE ASSISTANT COMMISSIONER FOR TRADEMARKS:

**APPLICANT'S NAME:** AMALGAMATED DANCERS' UNION, LOCAL 55, INC.

**APPLICANT'S MAILING ADDRESS:** 257 83RD ST.

(Display address exactly as it should appear on registration)
NEW YORK, NY 10011

### APPLICANT'S ENTITY TYPE: (Check one and supply requested information)

| | |
|---|---|
| | Individual - Citizen of (Country): |
| | Partnership - State where organized (Country, if appropriate): _____ Names and Citizenship (Country) of General Partners: _____ |
| X | Corporation - State (Country, if appropriate) of Incorporation:  NEW YORK |
| | Other (Specify Nature of Entity and Domicile): |

Applicant requests registration of the collective membership mark shown in the accompanying drawing in the United States Patent and Trademark Office on the Principal Register established by the Act of July 5, 1946 (15 U.S.C. 1051 et. seq., as amended) to indicate membership in a(n): _____

AMALGAMATED DANCERS' UNION, LOCAL 55, WHICH IS A LABOR UNION

(Specify the type or nature of the organization, for example, a social club, labor union, political society, or an association of real estate brokers.)

### BASIS FOR APPLICATION: (Check boxes which apply, but never both the first AND second boxes, and supply requested information related to each box checked.)

[ ]  Applicant is exercising legitimate control over the use of the mark in commerce by its members to indicate membership. (15 U.S.C. 1051(a) and 1054 as amended.) Three specimens showing the mark as used by the members in commerce are submitted with this application.
- Date of first use of the mark by members in commerce which the U.S. Congress may regulate (for example, interstate or between the U.S. and a specified foreign country): _____
- Specify the type of commerce: _____
  (for example, interstate or between the U.S. and a specified foreign country)
- Date of first use anywhere (the same as or before use in commerce date): _____
- Specify manner or method of using mark to indicate membership: _____

  (for example, mark is applied to membership cards, certificates, window decals)

[x]  Applicant has a bona fide intention to exercise legitimate control over the use of the mark in commerce by its members to indicate membership. (15 U.S.C. 1051(b) and 1054, as amended.)
- Specify intended manner or method of using mark to indicate membership _____
  MARK WILL BE EMBROIDERED PATCHES WORN ON DANCERS' TUTUS
  (for example, mark is applied to membership cards, certificates, window decals)

[ ]  Applicant has a bona fide intention to exercise legitimate control over the use of the mark in commerce by its members to indicate membership, and asserts a claim of priority based upon a foreign application in accordance with 15 U.S.C. 1126(d), as amended.
- Country of foreign filing: _____
- Date of foreign filing: _____

[ ]  Applicant has a bona fide intention to exercise legitimate control over the use of the mark in commerce by its members to indicate membership and, accompanying this application, submits a certification or certified copy of a foreign registration in accordance with 15 U.S.C 1126(e), as amended.
- Country of registration: _____
- Registration number: _____

**NOTE: Declaration, on Reverse Side, MUST be Signed**

PTO Form 4.8
OMB No. 0651-0009 (Exp. 06/30/98) There is no requirement to respond to this collection of information unless a currently valid OMB Number is displayed.
U.S. DEPARTMENT OF COMMERCE/Patent and Trademark Office

*form 6*

| CERTIFICATION MARK APPLICATION, PRINCIPAL REGISTER, WITH DECLARATION | MARK (Word(s) and/or Design)  F-L |
|---|---|
| | CLASS  [x] A. Goods    [ ] B. Services |

## TO THE ASSISTANT COMMISSIONER FOR TRADEMARKS:

**APPLICANT'S NAME:** FRED'S LABS, INC.

**APPLICANT'S MAILING ADDRESS:** 1209 EAST END RD.

(Display address exactly as it should appear on registration) SELMA, AL 30110

**APPLICANT'S ENTITY TYPE:** (Check one and supply requested information)

| | Individual - Citizen of (Country): |
|---|---|
| | Partnership - State where organized (Country, if appropriate): _____ Names and Citizenship (Country) of General Partners: _____ |
| X | Corporation - State (Country, if appropriate) of Incorporation:    ALABAMA |
| | Other (Specify Nature of Entity and Domicile): |

## GOODS AND/OR SERVICES:

Applicant requests registration of the certification mark shown in the accompanying drawing in the United States Patent and Trademark Office on the Principal Register established by the Act of July 5, 1946 (15 U.S.C. 1051 et. seq., as amended) for the following goods/services (**SPECIFIC GOODS AND/OR SERVICES MUST BE INSERTED HERE**): _____
ELECTRICAL APPLIANCES

The certification mark, as used (or, if filing under 15 U.S.C. 1051(b), intended to be used) by authorized persons, certifies (or, if filing under 15 U.S.C. 1051(b), is intended to certify): _____
IT HAS BEEN TESTED BY FRED'S LABS, INC. AND FOUND TO BE SAFE TO USE.
(for example, a particular regional origin of the goods, a characteristic of the goods or services, that labor was performed by a particular group)

## BASIS FOR APPLICATION: (Check boxes which apply, but never both the first AND second boxes, and supply requested information related to each box checked.)

| [x] | Applicant is exercising legitimate control over the use of the certification mark in commerce on or in connection with the above identified goods/services. (15 U.S.C. 1051(a) and 1054 as amended.) Three specimens showing the mark as used by authorized persons in commerce are submitted with this application. |
|---|---|
| | • Date of first use anywhere of the mark by authorized person in commerce which the U.S. Congress may regulate (for example, interstate or between the U.S. and a specified foreign country): ___ JANUARY 26, 1999 |
| | • Specify the type of commerce: ___ INTERSTATE ___ (for example, interstate or between the U.S. and a specified foreign country) |
| | • Date of first use anywhere by an authorized person (the same as or before use in commerce date): JANUARY 19, 1963 |
| | • Specify manner of using mark on or in connection with the goods/services: _____ MARK IS APPLIED TO LABELS ATTACHED TO THE GOODS (for example, trademark is applied to labels, service mark is used in advertisements) |
| [ ] | Applicant has a bona fide intention to exercise legitimate control over the use of the certification mark in commerce on or in connection with the above identified goods/services. (15 U.S.C. 1051(b) and 1054, as amended.) |
| | • Specify intended manner or method of using mark on or in connection with the goods/services: _____ (for example, trademark will be applied to labels, service mark will be used in advertisements) |
| [ ] | Applicant has a bona fide intention to exercise legitimate control over the use of the certification mark in commerce on or in connection with the above identified goods/services, and asserts a claim of priority based upon a foreign application in accordance with 15 U.S.C. 1126(d), as amended. |
| | • Country of foreign filing: _____ • Date of foreign filing: _____ |
| [ ] | Applicant has a bona fide intention to exercise legitimate control over the use of the certification mark in commerce on or in connection with the above identified goods/services and, accompanying this application, submits a certification or certified copy of a foreign registration in accordance with 15 U.S.C 1126(e), as amended. |
| | • Country of registration: _____ • Registration number: _____ |

| ALLEGATION OF USE FOR INTENT-TO-USE APPLICATION, WITH DECLARATION (Amendment To Allege Use/Statement Use) | MARK (Identify the mark)    SAHARA |
|---|---|
| | SERIAL NO.    135792468 |

## TO THE ASSISTANT COMMISSIONER FOR TRADEMARKS:

APPLICANT NAME:    MARTIN SAND

Applicant requests registration of the above-identified trademark/service mark in the United States Patent and Trademark Office on the Principal Register established by the Act of July 5, 1946 (15 U.S.C. §1051 *et seq.*, as amended).  Three specimens per class showing the mark as used in commerce and the prescribed fees are submitted with this statement.

**Applicant is using the mark in commerce on or in connection with the following goods/services (CHECK ONLY ONE):**

☒ (a) those in the application or Notice of Allowance; **OR**

☐ (b)  those in the application or Notice of Allowance **except** (if goods/services are to be deleted, list the goods/services to be **deleted**): _____

_____

Date of first use in commerce which the U.S. Congress may regulate: OCTOBER 25, 1998
Specify type of commerce: _____ INTERSTATE _____
                              (for example, interstate and/or commerce between the U.S. and a foreign country)
Date of first use anywhere: _____ OCTOBER 25, 1998 _____

Specify manner or mode of use of mark on or in connection with the goods/services: (for example, trademark is applied to labels, service mark is used in advertisements): _____
              MARK IS PRINTED ON THE FRONT OF THE GOODS

The undersigned, being hereby warned that willful false statements and the like so made are punishable by fine or imprisonment, or both, under 18 U.S.C. §1001, and that such willful false statements may jeopardize the validity of the application or any resulting registration, declares that he/she is properly authorized to execute this Amendment to Allege Use or Statement of Use on behalf of the applicant; he/she believes the applicant to be the owner of the trademark/service mark sought to be registered; the trademark /service mark is now in use in commerce; and all statements made of his/her own knowledge are true and all statements made on information and belief are believed to be true.

| October 31, 1998 | *Martin Sand* |
|---|---|
| Date | Signature |
| 908-555-1212 | MARTIN SAND |
| Telephone Number | Type or Print Name and Position |

    **Check here if Request to Divide is being submitted with this statement** (if Applicant wishes to proceed to publication or registration with certain goods/services on or in connection with which it has used the mark in commerce and retain an active application for any remaining goods/services, a divisional application and fee are required.  37 C.F.R. §2.87)

### PLEASE SEE REVERSE FOR MORE INFORMATION

PTO Form 1553
OMB No. 0651-000 (Exp. 06/30/98) There is no requirement to respond to this collection of information unless a currently valid OMB Number is displayed.
U.S. Department of Commerce/Patent and Trademark Office

123

| REQUEST FOR EXTENSION OF TIME TO FILE A STATEMENT OF USE, WITH DECLARATION | MARK (Identify the mark) | SPIDER |
|---|---|---|
| | SERIAL NO. | 2468013579 |

## TO THE ASSISTANT SECRETARY AND COMMISSIONER OF PATENTS AND TRADEMARKS:

APPLICANT NAME:     SPIDER WEBBING INC.

NOTICE OF ALLOWANCE MAILING DATE:   March 25, 1998

Applicant requests a six-month extension of time to file the Statement of Use under 37 CFR 2.89 in this application.

Applicant has a continued bona fide intention to use the mark in commerce on or in connection with the following goods/services: (Check One below)

☒ Those goods/services identified in the Notice of Allowance.

☐ Those goods/services identified in the Notice of Allowance except: (Identify goods/services to be **deleted** from application)

_____

_____

_____

This is the _____THIRD_____ request for an Extension of Time following mailing of the Notice of Allowance.
(Specify: First - Fifth)

If this is not the first request for an Extension of Time, check one box below. If the first box is checked explain the circumstance(s) of the non-use in the space provided:

☒ Applicant has not used the mark in commerce yet on all goods/services specified in the Notice of Allowance; however, applicant has made the following ongoing efforts to use the mark in commerce on or in connection with each of the goods/services specified above:

    THE MANUFACTURER HAD DELAYED IN DELIVERING SOME OF THE GOODS.
    SAID GOODS WILL BE USED IN COMMERCE AS SOON AS DELIVERED.

*If additional space is needed, please attach a separate sheet to this form*

☐ Applicant believes that it has made valid use of the mark in commerce, as evidenced by the Statement of Use submitted with this request; however, if the Statement of Use does not meet minimum requirements under 37 CFR 2.88(e), applicant will need additional time in which to file a new statement.

The undersigned being hereby warned that willful false statements and the like so made are punishable by fine or imprisonment, or both, under 18 U.S.C. 1001, and that such willful false statements may jeopardize the validity of the application or any resulting registration, declares that he/she is properly authorized to execute this Request for an Extension of Time to File a Statement of Use on behalf of the applicant; and that all statements made of his/her own knowledge are true and all statements made on information and belief are believed to be true.

_APRIL 2, 1999_         *Boris Spider*
Date                  Signature

_202-555-1212_        BORIS SPIDER, PRES.
Telephone Number        Type or Print Name and Position

    **Check here if Request to Divide is being submitted with this statement** (if Applicant wishes to proceed to publication or registration with certain goods/services on or in connection with which it has used the mark in commerce and retain an active application for any remaining goods/services, a divisional application and fee are required. 37 C.F.R. §2.87)

PTO Form 1581 (REV. 6-96)        U.S. Department of Commerce/Patent and Trademark Office
OMB No. 0651-0009
Exp. (06/30/98)    There is no requirement to respond to this collection of information unless a currently valid OMB Number is displayed

124

**TRADEMARK**

## UNITED STATES DEPARTMENT OF COMMERCE
## PATENT AND TRADEMARK OFFICE

Applicant SAM STREETCAR

Mark   JAYMEE

Serial Number   19234167

Filed    JANUARY 29, 1999

Trademark Law Office   D206

Trademark Attorney   STAN R. KUNTZ, III

Commissioner of Patents and Trademarks
Washington, D.C. 20231

### REQUEST TO DIVIDE APPLICATION

The applicant hereby requests that the application identified above be divided as follows:

Please retain in the original application the following goods/services—(use the language of the original application insofar as possible)

    BOOKS

Please include in the new, divided application the following goods/services—(They should be different from and should not overlap, those remaining in the original application.)

    AUDIO CASSETTES

(check one)

[x]    Enclosed is a check in payment of the filing fee for the divided application

[ ]    The divided application includes all goods or services in a single class presented in the original, parent application; therefore the applicant submits that no filing fee is due or required.

DATED: APRIL 2, 1999

Respectfully,

*Sam Streetcar*

Telephone Number: 202-555-1212
Address: 124 HERBERTSON RD., MUNDY, IL 12456

| DECLARATION OF USE OF A MARK UNDER **SECTION 8** OF THE TRADEMARK ACT OF 1946, AS AMENDED | MARK (Identify the mark) | PONY |
|---|---|---|
| | REGISTRATION NO. 14028800 | DATE OF REGISTRATION: SEPT. 6, 1995 |

**TO THE ASSISTANT SECRETARY AND COMMISSIONER OF PATENTS AND TRADEMARKS:**

REGISTRANT'S NAME:[1]   WILLIAM WILLIAMS

REGISTRANT'S CURRENT MAILING ADDRESS:   124 CHANOWIN LANE
MUNDY, IL 01234

**GOODS AND/OR SERVICES AND USE IN COMMERCE STATEMENT:**

The mark shown in Registration No. __14028800__ owned by the above-identified registrant is in use in

__INTERSTATE__ commerce on or in connection with all of the goods and/or services identified in the
 (type of)[2]

registration, (*except* for the following)[3] _____ NONE EXCEPTED _____

_____ ;

as evidenced by the attached specimen(s)[4] showing the mark as currently used.

**DECLARATION**

The undersigned being hereby warned that willful false statements and the like so made are punishable by fine or imprisonment, or both, under 18 U.S.C. 1001, and that such willful false statements may jeopardize the validity of this document, declares that he/she is properly authorized to execute this document on behalf of the registrant; he/she believes the registrant to be the owner of the above identified registration; the trademark/service mark is in use in commerce; and all statements made of his/her own knowledge are true and all statements made on information and belief are believed to be true.

OCT. 1, 2000
Date

*William Williams*
Signature

630-555-1212
Telephone Number

WILLIAM WILLIAMS
Print or Type Name and Position
[if applicable][5]

| DECLARATION OF INCONTESTABILITY OF A MARK UNDER **SECTION 15** OF THE TRADEMARK ACT OF 1946 AS AMENDED | MARK (Identify the mark) PONY | |
|---|---|---|
| | REGISTRATION NO. 14028800 | DATE OF REGISTRATION: SEPT. 6, 1995 |

**TO THE ASSISTANT SECRETARY AND COMMISSIONER OF PATENTS AND TRADEMARKS:**

REGISTRANT'S NAME:[1]    WILLIAM WILLIAMS

REGISTRANT'S CURRENT MAILING ADDRESS:    124 CHANOWIN LANE
MUNDY, IL 01234

GOODS AND/OR SERVICES AND USE IN COMMERCE STATEMENT:

The mark shown in **Principal Register** Registration No. _14028800_____, owned by the above-identified

registrant has been incontinuous use in ___INTERSTATE___ commerce for five consecutive years from ___SEPT. 6, 1995___
(type of)[2]                                            (date)

to the present on or in connection with all of the goods and/or services identified in the registration, (*except* for the following)[3]

_____NONE EXCEPTED_____

_____.

There has been no final decision adverse to registrant's claim of ownership of such mark for such goods or

services, or to registrant's right to register the same or to keep the same on the register; and there is no

proceeding involving said rights pending and not disposed of either in the Patent and Trademark Office or in

the courts.

DECLARATION

The undersigned being hereby warned that willful false statements and the like so made are punishable by fine or imprisonment, or both, under 18 U.S.C. 1001, and that such willful false statements may jeopardize the validity of this document, declares that he/she is properly authorized to execute this document on behalf of the registrant; he/she believes the registrant to be the owner of the above identified registration; the trademark/service mark is in use in commerce; and all statements made of his/her own knowledge are true and all statements made on information and belief are believed to be true.

OCT. 1, 2000
Date

630-555-1212
Telephone Number

*William Williams*
Signature

WILLIAM WILLIAMS
Print or Type Name and Position
[if applicable][4]

| COMBINED DECLARATION OF USE AND INCONTESTABILITY UNDER **SECTIONS 8 & 15**[1] OF THE TRADEMARK ACT OF 1946, AS AMENDED | MARK (Identify the mark) PONY | |
|---|---|---|
| | **REGISTRATION NO.** 14028800 | **DATE OF REGISTRATION:** SEPT. 6, 1995 |

TO THE ASSISTANT SECRETARY AND COMMISSIONER OF PATENTS AND TRADEMARKS:

REGISTRANT'S NAME:[2]   WILLIAM WILLIAMS

REGISTRANT'S CURRENT MAILING ADDRESS   124 CHANOWIN LANE
MUNDY, IL 01234

GOODS AND/OR SERVICES AND USE IN COMMERCE STATEMENT:

The mark shown in Registration No. _14028800_, owned by the above-identified registrant, has been in

continuous use in __INTERSTATE__commerce for five consecutive years from the date of registration or the
(type of)[3]

date of publication under §12(c)[4] to the present, on or in connection with all the goods and/or services

identified in the registration, (*except* for the following)[5] __NONE EXCEPTED__

_____ ;

as evidenced by the attached specimen(s)[6] showing the mark as currently used. There has been no final

decision adverse to registrant's claim of ownership of such mark for such goods or services, or to registrant's

right to register the same or to keep the same on the register; and there is no proceeding involving said

rights pending and not disposed of either in the Patent and Trademark Office or in the courts.

### DECLARATION

The undersigned being hereby warned that willful false statements and the like so made are punishable by fine or imprisonment, or both, under 18 U.S.C. 1001, and that such willful false statements may jeopardize the validity of this document, declares that he/she is properly authorized to execute this document on behalf of the registrant; he/she believes the registrant to be the owner of the above identified registration; the trademark/service mark is in use in commerce; and all statements made of his/her own knowledge are true and all statements made on information and belief are believed to be true.

__OCT. 1, 2000__
Date

__630-555-1212__
Telephone Number

*William Williams*
Signature

WILLIAM WILLIAMS
Print or Type Name and Position
[if applicable][5]

| APPLICATION FOR RENEWAL OF REGISTRATION OF A MARK UNDER SECTION 9 OF THE TRADEMARK ACT OF 1946, AS AMENDED | MARK (Identify the mark)        STAR |
|---|---|

| REGISTRATION NO. 34567890 | DATE OF REGISTRATION: JULY 5, 1989 |
|---|---|

## TO THE ASSISTANT SECRETARY AND COMMISSIONER OF PATENTS AND TRADEMARKS:

REGISTRANT'S NAME:[1]     JAMES SMITH, INCORPORATED

REGISTRANT'S CURRENT MAILING ADDRESS:     600 MAPLE AVE

CRESCENT CITY, IOWA 45678

## GOODS AND/OR SERVICES AND USE IN COMMERCE STATEMENT:

The mark shown in Registration No. _____34567890_____ owned by the above-identified registrant is still in use in

_____INTERSTATE_____ commerce on or in connection with all of the goods and/or services identified in the
(type of)[2]

registration, (*except* for the following)[3] _____ NONE EXCEPTED _____

as evidenced by the attached specimen(s)[4] showing the mark as currently used.

### DECLARATION

The undersigned being hereby warned that willful false statements and the like so made are punishable by fine or imprisonment, or both, under 18 U.S.C. 1001, and that such willful false statements may jeopardize the validity of this document, declares that he/she is properly authorized to execute this document on behalf of the registrant; he/she believes the registrant to be the owner of the above identified registration; the trademark/service mark is in use in commerce; and all statements made of his/her own knowledge are true and all statements made on information and belief are believed to be true.

_____AUGUST 10, 1999_____
Date

_____*James Smith*_____
Signature

_____510-555-1212_____
Telephone Number

_____JAMES SMITH, PRESIDENT_____
Print or Type Name and Position
[if applicable][5]

*form 14*

| DESIGNATION OF<br>DOMESTIC REPRESENTATIVE | MARK *(identify the mark)*<br>PERIODICO UNO |
| --- | --- |
| | REGISTRATION NO. (IF KNOWN)<br>23456789 |
| | CLASS NO. (S)<br>16 (U.S. 37 & 38) |

WILLIAM D. VAN PIPPERMORE III
_____
*(name of domestic representative)*

whose postal address is _____ 1001 AVENUE OF THE ATTORNEYS, NEW YORK, NY 10001 _____

_____ is hereby designated applicant's representative upon whom notice or process in proceedings affecting the mark may be served.

*William D. Van Pippermore III*
_____
*(signature of applicant or owner of mark)*

JULY 4, 1999
_____
*(date)*

| ASSIGNMENT OF REGISTRATION OF A MARK | MARK *(identify the mark)*  M+M |
|---|---|
| | REGISTRATION NO. (IF KNOWN)  12345678 |
| | CLASS NO. (S)  30 |

Whereas _____ MARY MAJORS _____

_____ *(name of assignor)*

whose postal address is _____ 123 CANTRAL AVE., WESTPORT ME 01212 _____

_____ has adopted, used and is using a mark which is registered in the

United States Patent and Trademark Office, Registration No. _____ 12345678 _____ dated

_____ JULY 17, 1973 _____; and whereas _____ MARCIA NOVAK _____

*(name of assignee)*

whose postal address is _____ 456 DUHME RD. FALLS CHURCH, VA 22044 _____

is desirous of acquiring said mark and the registration thereof;

Now, therefore, for good and valuable consideration, receipt of which is hereby acknowledged, said

_____ MARY MAJORS _____ does hereby assign unto the said

*(name of assignor)*

_____ MARCIA NOVAK _____ all right, title and interest in and to

*(name of assignee)*

the said mark, together with the good will of the business symbolized by the mark, and the above registration

thereof.


_____ *MARY MAJORS* _____

*(signature of assignor, if assignor is a corporation or other juristic organization give the official title of the person who signs for assignor)*


State of _____ MAINE _____ } ss.

County of _____ LEE _____

On this _1_ day of AUGUST _____, 19 _98_, before me appeared _MARY MAJORS_ _____

_____ the person who signed this instrument, who acknowledged that he/she

signed it as a free act on his/her own behalf (or on behalf of the identified corporation or other juristic entity

with authority to do so).*


_____ *C.U. Sine* _____

*(signature of notary public)*


* The wording of the acknowledgment may vary in some jurisdictions. Be sure to use wording acceptable in the jurisdiction where the document is executed.

*form 16*

FORM PTO-1618A
Expires 06/30/99
OMB 0651-0027

U.S. Department of Commerce
Patent and Trademark Office
**TRADEMARK**

# RECORDATION FORM COVER SHEET
# TRADEMARKS ONLY

TO: The Commissioner of Patents and Trademarks: Please record the attached original document(s) or copy(ies).

## Submission Type

[X] **New**

[ ] **Resubmission** **(Non-Recordation)**
Document ID # _____

[ ] **Correction of PTO Error**
Reel # _____  Frame # _____

[ ] **Corrective Document**
Reel # _____  Frame # _____

## Conveyance Type

[X] **Assignment**  [ ] **License**

[ ] **Security Agreement**  [ ] **Nunc Pro Tunc Assignment**

[ ] **Merger**

**Effective Date**
Month Day Year
| 06 | 05 | 99 |

[ ] **Change of Name**

[ ] **Other** _____

## Conveying Party

[ ] Mark if additional names of conveying parties attached

**Execution Date**
Month Day Year
| 06 | 05 | 99 |

Name | SPIDER WEBBING, INC. |

Formerly | |

[ ] **Individual**  [ ] **General Partnership**  [ ] **Limited Partnership**  [X] **Corporation**  [ ] **Association**

[ ] **Other** _____

[ ] **Citizenship/State of Incorporation/Organization** | DISTRICT OF COLUMBIA |

## Receiving Party

[ ] Mark if additional names of receiving parties attached

Name | WEB MASTER, INC. |

DBA/AKA/TA | |

Composed of | |

Address (line 1) | 123 MAIN ST. |

Address (line 2) | |

Address (line 3) | NAPERVILLE | IL | 60540 |
City | State/Country | Zip Code

[ ] **Individual**  [ ] **General Partnership**  [ ] **Limited Partnership**

[X] **Corporation**  [ ] **Association**

[ ] **Other** _____

If document to be recorded is an assignment and the receiving party is not domiciled in the United States, an appointment of a domestic representative should be attached. *(Designation must be a separate document from Assignment.)*

[ ] **Citizenship/State of Incorporation/Organization** | ILLINOIS |

### FOR OFFICE USE ONLY

Public burden reporting for this collection of information is estimated to average approximately 30 minutes per Cover Sheet to be recorded, including time for reviewing the document and gathering the data needed to complete the Cover Sheet. Send comments regarding this burden estimate to the U.S. Patent and Trademark Office, Chief Information Officer, Washington, D.C. 20231 and to the Office of Information and Regulatory Affairs, Office of Management and Budget, Paperwork Reduction Project (0651-0027), Washington, D.C. 20503. See OMB Information Collection Budget Package 0651-0027, Patent and Trademark Assignment Practice. DO NOT SEND REQUESTS TO RECORD ASSIGNMENT DOCUMENTS TO THIS ADDRESS.

**Mail documents to be recorded with required cover sheet(s) information to:**
**Commissioner of Patents and Trademarks, Box Assignments , Washington, D.C. 20231**

FORM PTO-1618B
Expires 06/30/99
OMB 0651-0027

U.S. Department of Commerce
Patent and Trademark Office
**TRADEMARK**

## Domestic Representative Name and Address    Enter for the first Receiving Party only.

| | |
|---|---|
| Name | |
| Address (line 1) | |
| Address (line 2) | |
| Address (line 3) | |
| Address (line 4) | |

## Correspondent Name and Address   Area Code and Telephone Number

| | |
|---|---|
| Name | |
| Address (line 1) | |
| Address (line 2) | |
| Address (line 3) | |
| Address (line 4) | |

**Pages**   Enter the total number of pages of the attached conveyance document including any attachments.   #

## Trademark Application Number(s) or Registration Number(s)   [X] Mark if additional numbers attached

*Enter either the Trademark Application Number or the Registration Number (DO NOT ENTER BOTH numbers for the same property).*

| Trademark Application Number(s) | | | Registration Number(s) | | |
|---|---|---|---|---|---|
| | | | 1234567 | 4567890 | 7890123 |
| | | | 2345678 | 5678901 | 8901234 |
| | | | 3456789 | 6789012 | 9012345 |

**Number of Properties**   Enter the total number of properties involved.   #   10

**Fee Amount**   Fee Amount for Properties Listed (37 CFR 3.41):   $   1,000.00

Method of Payment:   Enclosed [X]   Deposit Account [ ]

Deposit Account
(Enter for payment by deposit account or if additional fees can be charged to the account.)
Deposit Account Number:   #

Authorization to charge additional fees:   Yes [X]   No [ ]

## Statement and Signature

*To the best of my knowledge and belief, the foregoing information is true and correct and any attached copy is a true copy of the original document. Charges to deposit account are authorized, as indicated herein.*

| Boris Spider | *Boris Spider* | JUNE 5, 1999 |
|---|---|---|
| **Name of Person Signing** | **Signature** | **Date Signed** |

*form 18*

# RECORDATION FORM COVER SHEET
# CONTINUATION
# TRADEMARKS ONLY

FORM PTO-1618C
Expires 06/30/99
OMB 0651-0027

U.S. Department of Commerce
Patent and Trademark Office
**TRADEMARK**

## Conveying Party
Enter Additional Conveying Party

☐ Mark if additional names of conveying parties attached

**Execution Date**
Month  Day  Year

Name: SPIDER WEBBING, INC.

06  05  99

Formerly:

☐ Individual  ☐ General Partnership  ☐ Limited Partnership  ☒ Corporation  ☐ Association

☐ Other

☐ Citizenship State of Incorporation/Organization  DISTRICT OF COLUMBIA

## Receiving Party
Enter Additional Receiving Party

☐ Mark if additional names of receiving parties attached

Name: WEB MASTER, INC.

DBA/AKA/TA:

Composed of:

Address (line 1): 123 MAIN ST.

Address (line 2):

Address (line 3): NAPERVILLE | IL | 60540
City | State/Country | Zip Code

☐ Individual  ☐ General Partnership  ☐ Limited Partnership

☒ Corporation  ☐ Association

☐ Other

☐ If document to be recorded is an assignment and the receiving party is not domiciled in the United States, an appointment of a domestic representative should be attached (Designation must be a separate document from the Assignment.)

☐ Citizenship/State of Incorporation/Organization

## Trademark Application Number(s) or Registration Number(s)

☐ Mark if additional numbers attached

Enter either the Trademark Application Number or the Registration Number (DO NOT ENTER BOTH numbers for the same property).

| Trademark Application Number(s) | | | Registration Number(s) | | |
|---|---|---|---|---|---|
| | | | 0123456 | | |
| | | | | | |
| | | | | | |
| | | | | | |
| | | | | | |
| | | | | | |
| | | | | | |

Application to Record Trademark
with the United States Customs Service

To:     Intellectual Property Rights Branch
        U. S. Customs Service
        1301 Constitution Ave., N.W.
        Washington, DC 20229

Name of trademark owner: ATOM INDUSTRIES, INC

Address of trademark owner:

> 102 SUNSET BLVD.
> KEY WEST FLORIDA 33410

Trademark owner is:
- ☐ an individual who is a citizen of _____
- ☐ a partnership whose partners are citizens of _____
- ☒ an association or corporation which was organized under the laws of

    _____NEVADA_____

Places of manufacture of goods bearing the trademark:

> FLORIDA, USA

The following are foreign persons authorized to use the trademark:

Name: Address:                                    Use authorized:

> NONE

Identification of any foreign parent or subsidiaries under common ownership or control which uses the trademark abroad*:

> NONE

Include with this form:
1. A status copy of the certificate of registration certified by the U. S. Patent and Trademark Office showing title to be presently in the name of the applicant.
2. Five copies of the certificate or of a U. S. Patent and Trademark Office Certificate.
3. A fee of $190 for each class of goods sought to be protected.

*Note, "common ownership" means individual or aggregate ownership of more than 50% of the business entity and "common control" means effective control in policy and operations and is not necessarily synonymous with common ownership.

# APPENDIX C
# BLANK FORMS

The following pages contain the forms mentioned throughout this book. They may be either removed from this book and used, or photocopied. The forms are occasionally revised by the Patent and Trademark Office, but in most cases the previous versions of the forms are acceptable. If you would like to see if new versions of the forms are available you can check the Patent and Trademark Office website at http://www.uspto.gov/web/forms/

_____

[Your Name]

_____

[Address]

_____

[City, State Zip]

_____

[Phone]


[Date]


Hon Commissioner of Patents and Trademarks
Washington, DC 20231

Re: In Use Trademark Application


Sir:


Enclosed for filing please find trademark application papers of
_____ for the mark
"_____" in International Class _____ (Prior
U.S. Class _____) together with the drawing, three specimens and
the filing fee of $245.

A self-addressed, stamped envelope is enclosed for return of the
receipt.


Respectfully submitted,



_____

[Your Name]

_____

[Your Name]

_____

[Address]

_____

[City, State Zip]

_____

[Phone]

[Date]

Hon Commissioner of Patents and Trademarks
Washington, DC 20231

Re: Intent-to-Use Trademark Application

Sir:

Enclosed for filing please find trademark application papers of
_____ for the mark
"_____" in International Class _____ (Prior
U.S. Class _____) together with the drawing and the filing fee of
$245.

A self-addressed, stamped envelope is enclosed for return of the
receipt.

Respectfully submitted,

_____

[Your Name]

| TRADEMARK/SERVICE MARK APPLICATION, PRINCIPAL REGISTER, WITH DECLARATION | MARK (Word(s) and/or Design) | CLASS NO. (If known) |
|---|---|---|

## TO THE ASSISTANT COMMISSIONER FOR TRADEMARKS:

**APPLICANT'S NAME:**

**APPLICANT'S MAILING ADDRESS:**

(Display address exactly as it should appear on registration)

_____
_____
_____
_____

**APPLICANT'S ENTITY TYPE: (Check one and supply requested information)**

|  | Individual - Citizen of (Country): |
|---|---|
|  | Partnership - State where organized (Country, if appropriate): _____<br>Names and Citizenship (Country) of General Partners: _____ |
|  | Corporation - State (Country, if appropriate) of Incorporation: |
|  | Other (Specify Nature of Entity and Domicile): |

**GOODS AND/OR SERVICES:**

Applicant requests registration of the trademark/service mark shown in the accompanying drawing in the United States Patent and Trademark Office on the Principal Register established by the Act of July 5, 1946 (15 U.S.C. 1051 et. seq., as amended) for the following goods/services **(SPECIFIC GOODS AND/OR SERVICES MUST BE INSERTED HERE)**:

_____
_____
_____
_____
_____

**BASIS FOR APPLICATION:** (Check boxes which apply, **but never both the first AND second boxes,** and supply requested information related to each box checked.)

[ ] Applicant is using the mark in commerce on or in connection with the above identified goods/services. (15 U.S.C. 1051(a), as amended.) Three specimens showing the mark as used in commerce are submitted with this application.
- Date of first use of the mark in commerce which the U.S. Congress may regulate (for example, interstate or between the U.S. and a foreign country): _____
- Specify the type of commerce: _____
  (for example, interstate or between the U.S. and a specified foreign country)
- Date of first use anywhere (the same as or before use in commerce date): _____
- Specify intended manner or mode of use of mark on or in connection with the goods/services: _____

  (for example, trademark is applied to labels, service mark is used in advertisements)

[ ] Applicant has a bona fide intention to use the mark in commerce on or in connection with the above identified goods/services. (15 U.S.C. 1051(b), as amended.)
- Specify manner or mode of use of mark on or in connection with the goods/services: _____

  (for example, trademark will be applied to labels, service mark will be used in advertisements)

[ ] Applicant has a bona fide intention to use the mark in commerce on or in connection with the above identified goods/services, and asserts a claim of priority based upon a foreign application in accordance with 15 U.S.C. 1126(d), as amended.
- Country of foreign filing: _____     • Date of foreign filing: _____

[ ] Applicant has a bona fide intention to use the mark in commerce on or in connection with the above identified goods/services and, accompanying this application, submits a certification or certified copy of a foreign registration in accordance with 15 U.S.C 1126(e), as amended.
- Country of registration: _____     • Registration number: _____

## NOTE: Declaration, on Reverse Side, MUST be Signed

PTO Form 1478 (REV 6/96)                                                    U.S. DEPARTMENT OF COMMERCE/Patent and Trademark Office
OMB No. 0651-0009 (Exp. 06/30/98) There is no requirement to respond to this collection of information unless a currently valid OMB Number is displayed.

# DECLARATION

The undersigned being hereby warned that willful false statements and the like so made are punishable by fine or imprisonment, or both, under 18 U.S.C. 1001, and that such willful false statements may jeopardize the validity of the application or any resulting registration, declares that he/she is properly authorized to execute this application on behalf of the applicant; he/she believes the applicant to be the owner of the trademark/service mark sought to be registered, or if the application is being filed under 15 U.S.C. 1051(b), he/she believes the applicant to be entitled to use such mark in commerce; to the best of his/her knowledge and belief no other person, firm, corporation, or association has the right to use the above identified mark in commerce, either in the identical form thereof or in such near resemblance thereto as to be likely, when used on or in connection with the goods/services of such other person, to cause confusion, or to cause mistake, or to deceive; and that all statements made of his/her own knowledge are true and that all statements made on information and belief are believed to be true.

_____
DATE

_____
SIGNATURE

_____
TELEPHONE NUMBER

_____
PRINT OR TYPE NAME AND POSITION

## INSTRUCTIONS AND INFORMATION FOR APPLICANT

**TO RECEIVE A FILING DATE, THE APPLICATION MUST BE COMPLETED AND SIGNED BY THE APPLICANT AND SUBMITTED ALONG WITH:**

1.  The prescribed **FEE ($245.00)** for each class of goods/services listed in the application;
2.  A **DRAWING PAGE** displaying the mark in conformance with 37 CFR 2.52;
3.  If the application is based on use of the mark in commerce, **THREE (3) SPECIMENS** (evidence) of the mark as used in commerce for each class of goods/services listed in the application. All three specimens may be the same. Examples of good specimens include: (a) labels showing the mark which are placed on the goods; (b) photographs of the mark as it appears on the goods, (c) brochures or advertisements showing the mark as used in connection with the services.
4.  An **APPLICATION WITH DECLARATION** (this form) - The application must be signed in order for the application to receive a filing date. Only the following persons may sign the declaration, depending on the applicant's legal entity: (a) the individual applicant; (b) an officer of the corporate applicant; (c) one general partner of a partnership applicant; (d) all joint applicants.

**SEND APPLICATION FORM, DRAWING PAGE, FEE, AND SPECIMENS (IF APPROPRIATE) TO:**

**Assistant Commissioner for Trademarks**
**Box New App/Fee**
**2900 Crystal Drive**
**Arlington, VA 22202-3513**

Additional information concerning the requirements for filing an application is available in a booklet entitled **Basic Facts About Registering a Trademark,** which may be obtained by writing to the above address or by calling: (703) 308-HELP.

| COLLECTIVE TRADEMARK/SERVICE MARK APPLICATION, PRINCIPAL REGISTER, WITH DECLARATION | MARK (Word(s) and/or Design) | CLASS NO. (If known) |
|---|---|---|

## TO THE ASSISTANT COMMISSIONER FOR TRADEMARKS:

**APPLICANT'S NAME:**

**APPLICANT'S MAILING ADDRESS:** _____

(Display address exactly as it should appear on registration)  _____

_____

_____

**APPLICANT'S ENTITY TYPE: (Check one and supply requested information)**

| | |
|---|---|
| | Individual - Citizen of (Country): |
| | Partnership - State where organized (Country, if appropriate): _____ <br> Names and Citizenship (Country) of General Partners: _____ <br> _____ <br> _____ |
| | Corporation - State (Country, if appropriate) of Incorporation: |
| | Other (Specific Nature of Entity and Domicile): |

## GOODS AND/OR SERVICES:

Applicant requests registration of the collective mark shown in the accompanying drawing in the United States Patent and Trademark Office on the Principal Register established by the Act of July 5, 1946 (15 U.S.C. 1051 et. seq., as amended) for the following goods/services **(SPECIFIC GOODS AND/OR SERVICES MUST BE INSERTED HERE):** _____

_____

_____

_____

## BASIS FOR APPLICATION: (Check boxes which apply, but never both the first AND second boxes, and supply requested information related to each box checked.)

| | |
|---|---|
| [ ] | Applicant is exercising legitimate control over the use of the mark in commerce by its members on or in connection with the above identified goods/services. (15 U.S.C. 1051 (a) and 1054, as amended.) Three specimens showing the mark as used by the members in commerce are submitted with this application. <br><br> • Date of first use of the mark in commerce which the U.S. Congress may regulate (for example, interstate or between the U.S. and a foreign country): _____ <br> • Specify the type of commerce: _____ <br> (for example, interstate or between the U.S. and a specified foreign country) <br> • Date of first use anywhere (the same as or before use in commerce date): <br> • Specify intended manner or mode of use of mark on or in connection with the goods/services:_____ <br> (for example, trademark is applied to labels, service mark is used in advertisements) |
| [ ] | Applicant has a bona fide intention to exercise legitimate control over the use of the mark in commerce by its members on or in connection with the above-identified good/services. (15 U.S. C. 1051(b) and 1054, as amended.) <br> • Specify intended manner or mode of use of mark on or in connection with the goods/services: _____ <br> (for example, trademark will be applied to labels, service mark will be used in advertisements) |
| [ ] | Applicant has a bona fide intention to exercise legitimate control over the use of the mark in commerce by its members on or in connection with the above identified goods/services, and asserts a claim of priority based upon a foreign application in accordance with 15 U.S.C. 1126(d), as amended. <br> • Country of foreign filing: _____ • Date of foreign filing: _____ |
| [ ] | Applicant has a bona fide intention to exercise legitimate control over the use of the mark in commerce by its members on or in connection with the above identified goods/services and, accompanying this application, submits a certification or certified copy of a foreign registration in accordance with 15 U.S.C 1126(e), as amended. <br> • Country of registration: _____ • Registration number: _____ |

### NOTE: Declaration, on Reverse Side, MUST be Signed

PTO Form 1478(a) (REV 6/96)

OMB No. 0651-0009 (Exp. 06/30/98) There is no requirement to respond to this collection of information unless a currently valid OMB Number is displayed.

U.S. DEPARTMENT OF COMMERCE/Patent and Trademark Office

Applicant controls (or, if the application is being filed under 15 U.S.C. 1051(b), applicant intends to control) the use of the mark by the members in the following manner: _____

_____

_____

_____

NOTE: If applicant's bylaws or other written provisions specify the manner of control, or intended manner of control, it will be sufficient to state such bylaws or other written provisions.

## DECLARATION

The undersigned being hereby warned that willful false statements and the like so made are punishable by fine or imprisonment, or both, under 18 U.S.C. 1001, and that such willful false statements may jeopardize the validity of the application or any resulting registration, declares that he/she is properly authorized to execute this application on behalf of the applicant; he/she believes the applicant to be the owner of the mark sought to be registered, or, if the application is being filed under 15 U.S.C. 1051(b), he/she believes applicant is entitled to exercise legitimate control over use of the mark in commerce; to the best of his/her knowledge and belief no other person, firm, corporation, or association has the right to use the above identified mark in commerce, either in the identical form thereof or in such near resemblance thereto as to be likely, when used on or in connection with the goods/services of such other person, to cause confusion, or to cause mistake, or to deceive; and that all statements made of his/her own knowledge are true and that all statements made on information and belief are believed to be true.

_____

DATE

_____

TELEPHONE NUMBER

_____

SIGNATURE

_____

PRINT OR TYPE NAME AND POSITION

## INSTRUCTIONS AND INFORMATION FOR APPLICANT

**TO RECEIVE A FILING DATE, THE APPLICATION <u>MUST</u> BE COMPLETED AND SIGNED BY THE APPLICANT AND SUBMITTED ALONG WITH:**

1. The prescribed **FEE ($245.00)** for each class of goods/services listed in the application (**please note that fees are subject to change usually on October 1 of each year)**;
2. A **DRAWING PAGE** displaying the mark in conformance with 37 CFR 2.52;
3. If the application is based on use of the mark in commerce, **THREE (3) SPECIMENS** (evidence) of the mark as used by members in commerce. All three specimens may be the same and may be in the nature of: (a) labels showing the mark which are placed on the goods; (b) photographs of the marks as it appears on the goods, (c) brochures or advertisements showing the mark as used in connection with the services.
4. An **APPLICATION WITH DECLARATION** (this form) - The application must be signed in order for the application to receive a filing date. Only the following persons may sign the declaration: (a) the individual applicant; (b) an officer of the corporate applicant; (c) one general partner of a partnership applicant; (d) all joint applicants.

**SEND APPLICATION FORM, DRAWING PAGE, FEE, AND SPECIMENS (IF APPROPRIATE) TO:**

**Assistant Commissioner for Trademarks**
**Box New App/Fee**
**2900 Crystal Drive**
**Arlington, VA 22202-3513**

Additional information concerning the requirements for filing an application is available in a booklet entitled **Basic Facts About Registering a Trademark,** which may be obtained by writing to the above address or by calling: (703) 308-9000.

This form is estimated to take an average of 1 hour to complete, including time required for reading and understanding instructions, gathering necessary information, recordkeeping, and actually providing the information. Any comments on this form, including the amount of time required to complete this form, should be sent to the Office of Management and Organization, U.S. Patent and Trademark Office, U.S. Department of Commerce, Washington, D.C. 20231. Do NOT send completed forms to this address.

<table>
<tr>
<td>COLLECTIVE MEMBERSHIP MARK<br>APPLICATION, PRINCIPAL<br>REGISTER, WITH DECLARATION</td>
<td>MARK (Word(s) and/or Design)</td>
<td>CLASS NO. 200</td>
</tr>
</table>

## TO THE ASSISTANT COMMISSIONER FOR TRADEMARKS:

APPLICANT'S NAME:

APPLICANT'S MAILING ADDRESS: _____

(Display address exactly as it
should appear on registration)

_____

_____

_____

### APPLICANT'S ENTITY TYPE: (**Check one** and supply requested information)

| | |
|---|---|
| [ ] | Individual - Citizen of (Country): |
| [ ] | Partnership - State where organized (Country, if appropriate): _____<br>Names and Citizenship (Country) of General Partners: _____ |
| [ ] | Corporation - State (Country, if appropriate) of Incorporation: |
| [ ] | Other (Specify Nature of Entity and Domicile): |

Applicant requests registration of the collective membership mark shown in the accompanying drawing in the United States Patent and Trademark Office on the Principal Register established by the Act of July 5, 1946 (15 U.S.C. 1051 et. seq., as amended) to indicate membership in a(n): _____

_____

_____

(Specify the type or nature of the organization, for example, a social club, labor union, political society, or an association of real estate brokers.)

### BASIS FOR APPLICATION: (Check boxes which apply, **but never both the first AND second boxes,** and supply requested information related to each box checked.)

[ ] Applicant is exercising legitimate control over the use of the mark in commerce by its members to indicate membership. (15 U.S.C. 1051(a) and 1054 as amended.) Three specimens showing the mark as used by the members in commerce are submitted with this application.
- Date of first use of the mark by members in commerce which the U.S. Congress may regulate (for example, interstate or between the U.S. and a specified foreign country): _____
- Specify the type of commerce: _____
  (for example, interstate or between the U.S. and a specified foreign country)
- Date of first use anywhere (the same as or before use in commerce date): _____
- Specify manner or method of using mark to indicate membership: _____

  (for example, mark is applied to membership cards, certificates, window decals)

[ ] Applicant has a bona fide intention to exercise legitimate control over the use of the mark in commerce by its members to indicate membership. (15 U.S.C. 1051(b) and 1054, as amended.)
- Specify intended manner or method of using mark to indicate membership _____

  (for example, mark is applied to membership cards, certificates, window decals)

[ ] Applicant has a bona fide intention to exercise legitimate control over the use of the mark in commerce by its members to indicate membership, and asserts a claim of priority based upon a foreign application in accordance with 15 U.S.C. 1126(d), as amended.
- Country of foreign filing: _____
- Date of foreign filing: _____

[ ] Applicant has a bona fide intention to exercise legitimate control over the use of the mark in commerce by its members to indicate membership and, accompanying this application, submits a certification or certified copy of a foreign registration in accordance with 15 U.S.C 1126(e), as amended.
- Country of registration: _____
- Registration number: _____

### NOTE: Declaration, on Reverse Side, MUST be Signed

PTO Form 4.8
OMB No. 0651-0009 (Exp. 06/30/98) There is no requirement to respond to this collection of information unless a currently valid OMB Number is displayed.

U.S. DEPARTMENT OF COMMERCE/Patent and Trademark Office

Applicant is not engaged (or, if filing under 15 U.S.C 1051(b), will not engage) in the production or marketing of the goods or services to which the mark is applied.

The applicant must also provide a copy of the standards the applicant uses to determine whether goods or services will be certified. If the applicant files based on prior use in commerce, this should be provided with this application. In an application filed based on an intent to use in commerce, this should be provided with the Allegation of Use (Amendment to Allege Use/Statement of Use).

## DECLARATION

The undersigned being hereby warned that willful false statements and the like so made are punishable by fine or imprisonment, or both, under 18 U.S.C. 1001, and that such willful false statements may jeopardize the validity of the application or any resulting registration, declares that he/she is properly authorized to execute this application on behalf of the applicant; he/she believes the applicant to be the owner of the membership mark sought to be registered, or, if the application is being filed under 15 U.S.C. 1051(b), he/she believes applicant is entitled to exercise legitimate control over use of the mark in commerce; to the best of his/her knowledge and belief no other person, firm, corporation, or association has the right to use the above identified mark in commerce, either in the identical form thereof or in such near resemblance thereto as to be likely, when used on or in connection with the goods/services of such other person, to cause confusion, or to cause mistake, or to deceive; and that all statements made of his/her own knowledge are true and that all statements made on information and belief are believed to be true.

_____
DATE

_____
SIGNATURE

_____
TELEPHONE NUMBER

_____
PRINT OR TYPE NAME AND POSITION

## INSTRUCTIONS AND INFORMATION FOR APPLICANT

**TO RECEIVE A FILING DATE, THE APPLICATION MUST BE COMPLETED AND SIGNED BY THE APPLICANT AND SUBMITTED ALONG WITH:**

1. The prescribed **FEE ($245.00)** for each class of goods/services listed in the application (**please note that fees are subject to change usually on October 1 of each year**);
2. A **DRAWING PAGE** displaying the mark in conformance with 37 CFR 2.52;
3. If the application is based on use of the mark in commerce, **THREE (3) SPECIMENS** (evidence) of the mark as used in commerce for each class of goods/services listed in the application. All three specimens may be in the nature of: (a) labels showing the mark which are placed on the goods; (b) photographs of the mark as it appears on the goods, (c) brochures or advertisements showing the mark as used in connection with the services.
4. An **APPLICATION WITH DECLARATION** (this form) - The application must be signed in order for the application to receive a filing date. Only the following persons may sign the declaration: (a) the individual applicant; (b) an officer of the corporate applicant; (c) one general partner of a partnership applicant; (d) all joint applicants.

**SEND APPLICATION FORM, DRAWING PAGE, FEE, SPECIMENS (IF APPROPRIATE) AND COPY OF STANDARDS TO:**

**Assistant Commissioner for Trademarks**
**Box New App/Fee**
**2900 Crystal Drive**
**Arlington, VA 22202-3513**

Additional information concerning the requirements for filing an application is available in a booklet entitled **Basic Facts About Registering a Trademark,** which may be obtained by writing to the above address or by calling: (703) 308-9000.

| CERTIFICATION MARK APPLICATION, PRINCIPAL REGISTER, WITH DECLARATION | MARK (Word(s) and/or Design) |
|---|---|
| | CLASS          [ ] A. Goods          [ ] B. Services |

## TO THE ASSISTANT COMMISSIONER FOR TRADEMARKS:

**APPLICANT'S NAME:**

**APPLICANT'S MAILING ADDRESS:** _____

(Display address exactly as it should appear on registration) _____

_____

**APPLICANT'S ENTITY TYPE:** (**Check one** and supply requested information)

| | Individual - Citizen of (Country): |
|---|---|
| | Partnership - State where organized (Country, if appropriate): _____ <br> Names and Citizenship (Country) of General Partners: _____ |
| | Corporation - State (Country, if appropriate) of Incorporation: |
| | Other (Specify Nature of Entity and Domicile): |

## GOODS AND/OR SERVICES:

Applicant requests registration of the certification mark shown in the accompanying drawing in the United States Patent and Trademark Office on the Principal Register established by the Act of July 5, 1946 (15 U.S.C. 1051 et. seq., as amended) for the following goods/services (**SPECIFIC GOODS AND/OR SERVICES MUST BE INSERTED HERE**): _____

_____

_____

_____

The certification mark, as used (or, if filing under 15 U.S.C. 1051(b), intended to be used) by authorized persons, certifies (or, if filing under 15 U.S.C. 1051(b), is intended to certify): _____

(for example, a particular regional origin of the goods, a characteristic of the goods or services, that labor was performed by a particular group)

## BASIS FOR APPLICATION: (Check boxes which apply, **but never both the first AND second boxes,** and supply requested information related to each box checked.)

| [ ] | Applicant is exercising legitimate control over the use of the certification mark in commerce on or in connection with the above identified goods/services. (15 U.S.C. 1051(a) and 1054 as amended.) Three specimens showing the mark as used by authorized persons in commerce are submitted with this application. <br> • Date of first use anywhere of the mark by authorized person in commerce which the U.S. Congress may regulate (for example, interstate or between the U.S. and a specified foreign country): _____ <br> • Specify the type of commerce: _____ <br>     (for example, interstate or between the U.S. and a specified foreign country) <br> • Date of first use anywhere by an authorized person (the same as or before use in commerce date): _____ <br> • Specify manner of using mark on or in connection with the goods/services: _____ <br><br>     (for example, trademark is applied to labels, service mark is used in advertisements) |
|---|---|
| [ ] | Applicant has a bona fide intention to exercise legitimate control over the use of the certification mark in commerce on or in connection with the above identified goods/services. (15 U.S.C. 1051(b) and 1054, as amended.) <br> • Specify intended manner or method of using mark on or in connection with the goods/services: _____ <br><br>     (for example, trademark will be applied to labels, service mark will be used in advertisements) |
| [ ] | Applicant has a bona fide intention to exercise legitimate control over the use of the certification mark in commerce on or in connection with the above identified goods/services, and asserts a claim of priority based upon a foreign application in accordance with 15 U.S.C. 1126(d), as amended. <br> • Country of foreign filing: _____        • Date of foreign filing: _____ |
| [ ] | Applicant has a bona fide intention to exercise legitimate control over the use of the certification mark in commerce on or in connection with the above identified goods/services and, accompanying this application, submits a certification or certified copy of a foreign registration in accordance with 15 U.S.C 1126(e), as amended. <br> • Country of registration: _____        • Registration number: _____ |

PTO Form 4.9

OMB No. 0651-0009 (Exp. 06/30/98) There is no requirement to respond to this collection of information unless a currently valid OMB Number is displayed.

U.S. DEPARTMENT OF COMMERCE/Patent and Trademark Office

Applicant controls (or, if the application is being filed under 15 U.S.C. 1051(b), applicant intends to control) the use of the mark by the members in the following manner: _____

_____

_____

_____

NOTE: If applicant's bylaws or other written provisions specify the manner of control, or intended manner of control, it will be sufficient to state such bylaws or other written provisions.

## DECLARATION

The undersigned being hereby warned that willful false statements and the like so made are punishable by fine or imprisonment, or both, under 18 U.S.C. 1001, and that such willful false statements may jeopardize the validity of the application or any resulting registration, declares that he/she is properly authorized to execute this application on behalf of the applicant; he/she believes the applicant to be the owner of the mark sought to be registered, or, if the application is being filed under 15 U.S.C. 1051(b), he/she believes applicant is entitled to exercise legitimate control over use of the mark in commerce; to the best of his/her knowledge and belief no other person, firm, corporation, or association has the right to use the above identified mark in commerce, either in the identical form thereof or in such near resemblance thereto as to be likely, when used on or in connection with the goods/services of such other person, to cause confusion, or to cause mistake, or to deceive; and that all statements made of his/her own knowledge are true and that all statements made on information and belief are believed to be true.

_____          _____
DATE                                                SIGNATURE


_____          _____
TELEPHONE NUMBER                                    PRINT OR TYPE NAME AND POSITION

## INSTRUCTIONS AND INFORMATION FOR APPLICANT

**TO RECEIVE A FILING DATE, THE APPLICATION <u>MUST</u> BE COMPLETED AND SIGNED BY THE APPLICANT AND SUBMITTED ALONG WITH:**

1. The prescribed **FEE ($245.00)** for each class of goods/services listed in the application (**please note that fees are subject to change usually on October 1 of each year**);
2. A **DRAWING PAGE** displaying the mark in conformance with 37 CFR 2.52;
3. If the application is based on use of the mark in commerce, **THREE (3) SPECIMENS** (evidence) of the mark as used by members in commerce. All three specimens may be the same and may be in the nature of: (a) labels showing the mark which are placed on the goods; (b) photographs of the marks as it appears on the goods, (c) brochures or advertisements showing the mark as used in connection with the services.
4. An **APPLICATION WITH DECLARATION** (this form) - The application must be signed in order for the application to receive a filing date. Only the following person may sign the declaration: (a) the individual applicant; (b) an officer of the corporate applicant; (c) one general partner of a partnership applicant; (d) all joint applicants.

**SEND APPLICATION FORM, DRAWING PAGE, FEE, AND SPECIMENS (IF APPROPRIATE) TO:**

**Assistant Commissioner for Trademarks**
**Box New App/Fee**
**2900 Crystal Drive**
**Arlington, VA 22202-3513**

Additional information concerning the requirements for filing an application is available in a booklet entitled **Basic Facts About Registering a Trademark,** which may be obtained by writing to the above address or by calling: (703) 308-9000.

This form is estimated to take an average of 1 hour to complete, including time required for reading and understanding instructions, gathering necessary information, recordkeeping, and actually providing the information. Any comments on this form, including the amount of time required to complete this form, should be sent to the Office of Management and Organization, U.S. Patent and Trademark Office, U.S. Department of Commerce, Washington, D.C. 20231. Do NOT send completed forms to this address.

| ALLEGATION OF USE FOR INTENT-TO-USE APPLICATION, WITH DECLARATION (Amendment To Allege Use/Statement Use) | MARK (Identify the mark) |
|---|---|
| | SERIAL NO. |

## TO THE ASSISTANT COMMISSIONER FOR TRADEMARKS:

APPLICANT NAME:

Applicant requests registration of the above-identified trademark/service mark in the United States Patent and Trademark Office on the Principal Register established by the Act of July 5, 1946 (15 U.S.C. §1051 *et seq.*, as amended). Three specimens per class showing the mark as used in commerce and the prescribed fees are submitted with this statement.

**Applicant is using the mark in commerce on or in connection with the following goods/services (CHECK ONLY ONE):**

☐ (a) those in the application or Notice of Allowance; **OR**

☐ (b) those in the application or Notice of Allowance **except** (if goods/services are to be deleted, list the goods/services to be **deleted**): _____

_____

_____

Date of first use in commerce which the U.S. Congress may regulate: _____

Specify type of commerce: _____
    (for example, interstate and/or commerce between the U.S. and a foreign country)

Date of first use anywhere: _____

Specify manner or mode of use of mark on or in connection with the goods/services: (for example, trademark is applied to labels, service mark is used in advertisements): _____

_____

_____

The undersigned, being hereby warned that willful false statements and the like so made are punishable by fine or imprisonment, or both, under 18 U.S.C. §1001, and that such willful false statements may jeopardize the validity of the application or any resulting registration, declares that he/she is properly authorized to execute this Amendment to Allege Use or Statement of Use on behalf of the applicant; he/she believes the applicant to be the owner of the trademark/service mark sought to be registered; the trademark /service mark is now in use in commerce; and all statements made of his/her own knowledge are true and all statements made on information and belief are believed to be true.

_____          _____
Date                                     Signature

_____          _____
Telephone Number                         Type or Print Name and Position

**Check here if Request to Divide is being submitted with this statement** (if Applicant wishes to proceed to publication or registration with certain goods/services on or in connection with which it has used the mark in commerce and retain an active application for any remaining goods/services, a divisional application and fee are required. 37 C.F.R. §2.87)

### PLEASE SEE REVERSE FOR MORE INFORMATION

PTO Form 1553                                            U.S. Department of Commerce/Patent and Trademark Office
OMB No. 0651-000 (Exp. 06/30/98) There is no requirement to respond to this collection of information unless a currently valid OMB Number is displayed.

# INSTRUCTIONS AND INFORMATION FOR APPLICANT

In an application based upon a bona fide intention to use a mark in commerce, **the Applicant must use its mark in commerce before a registration will be issued.** After use begins, the applicant must file the Allegation of Use. If the Allegation of Use is filed before the mark is approved for publication in the *Official Gazette* it is treated under the statute as **an Amendment to Allege Use (AAU).** If it is filed after the Notice of Allowance is issued, it is treated under the statute as **a Statement of Use (SOU).** The Allegation of Use cannot be filed during the time period between approval of the mark for publication in the *Official Gazette* and the issuance of the Notice of Allowance. The difference between the AAU and SOU is the time at which each is filed during the process.

Additional requirements for filing this Allegation of Use:

1) the fee of $100.00 per class of goods/services **(please note that fees are subject to change, usually on October 1 of each year)**; and
2) three (3) specimens of the mark as used in commerce for each class of goods/services (for example, photographs of the mark as it appears on the goods, labels for affixation on goods, advertisements showing the mark as used in connection with services).

• The Applicant may list dates of use for one item in each class of goods/services identified in the Allegation of Use. The Applicant must have used the mark in commerce on all the goods/services in the class, however, it is only necessary to list the dates of use for one item in each class.

• Only the following persons may sign the verification on this form: (a) the individual applicant; (b) an officer of a corporate applicant; (c) one general partner of a partnership applicant; (d) all joint applicants.

• The goods/services in the Allegation of Use must be the same as those specified in the application or Notice of Allowance. The Applicant may limit or clarify the goods/services, but cannot add to or otherwise expand the identification specified in the application or Notice of Allowance. If goods/services are deleted, they may **not** be reinserted at a later time.

• Amendments to Allege Use are governed by Trademark Act §1(c), 15 U.S.C. §1051(c) and Trademark Rule 2.76, 37 C.F.R. §2.76. Statements of Use are governed by Trademark Act §1(d), 15 U.S.C. §1051(d) and Trademark Rule 2.88, 37 C.F.R. §2.88.

> **MAIL COMPLETED FORM TO:**
>
> **ASSISTANT COMMISSIONER FOR TRADEMARKS**
> **BOX AAU/SOU**
> **2900 CRYSTAL DRIVE**
> **ARLINGTON, VIRGINIA 22202-3513**

Please note that the filing date of a document in the Patent and Trademarks Office is the date of receipt in the Office, not the date of deposit of the mail. 37 C.F.R. §1.6. To avoid lateness due to mail delay, use of the certificate of mailing set forth below, is encouraged.

## COMBINED CERTIFICATE OF MAILING/CHECKLIST

Before filing this form, please make sure to complete the following:

- ☐ three specimens, per class have been enclosed;
- ☐ the filing fee of $100 (subject to change as noted above), per class has been enclosed; and
- ☐ the declaration has been signed by the appropriate party

## CERTIFICATE OF MAILING

I do hereby certify that the foregoing are being **deposited** with the United States Postal Service as first class mail, postage prepaid, in an envelope addressed to the Assistant Commissioner for Trademarks, 2900 Crystal Drive, Arlington, VA 22202-3513, on _____ (date).

_____        _____
Signature                               Date of Deposit

_____
Print or Type Name of Person Signing Certificate

This form is estimated to take 15 minutes to complete including time required for reading and understanding instructions, gathering necessary information, record keeping and actually providing the information. Any comments on the amount of time you require to complete this form should be sent to the Office of Management and Organization, U.S. Patent and Trademark Office, U.S. Department of Commerce, Washington, D.C. 20231. Do not send forms to this address.

| REQUEST FOR EXTENSION OF TIME TO FILE A STATEMENT OF USE, WITH DECLARATION | MARK (Identify the mark) |
|---|---|
| | SERIAL NO. |

## TO THE ASSISTANT SECRETARY AND COMMISSIONER OF PATENTS AND TRADEMARKS:

APPLICANT NAME:

NOTICE OF ALLOWANCE MAILING DATE:

Applicant requests a six-month extension of time to file the Statement of Use under 37 CFR 2.89 in this application.

Applicant has a continued bona fide intention to use the mark in commerce on or in connection with the following goods/services: (Check One below)

☐ Those goods/services identified in the Notice of Allowance.

☐ Those goods/services identified in the Notice of Allowance except: (Identify goods/services to be **deleted** from application)

_____

_____

_____

This is the_____ request for an Extension of Time following mailing of the Notice of Allowance.
      (Specify: First - Fifth)

If this is not the first request for an Extension of Time, check one box below. If the first box is checked explain the circumstance(s) of the non-use in the space provided:

☐    Applicant has not used the mark in commerce yet on all goods/services specified in the Notice of Allowance; however, applicant has made the following ongoing efforts to use the mark in commerce on or in connection with each of the goods/services specified above:

_____

_____

If additional space is needed, please attach a separate sheet to this form

☐    Applicant believes that it has made valid use of the mark in commerce, as evidenced by the Statement of Use submitted with this request; however, if the Statement of Use does not meet minimum requirements under 37 CFR 2.88(e), applicant will need additional time in which to file a new statement.

The undersigned being hereby warned that willful false statements and the like so made are punishable by fine or imprisonment, or both, under 18 U.S.C. 1001, and that such willful false statements may jeopardize the validity of the application or any resulting registration, declares that he/she is properly authorized to execute this Request for an Extension of Time to File a Statement of Use on behalf of the applicant; and that all statements made of his/her own knowledge are true and all statements made on information and belief are believed to be true.

_____        _____

Date                                                Signature

_____        _____

Telephone Number                          Type or Print Name and Position

    **Check here if Request to Divide is being submitted with this statement** (if Applicant wishes to proceed to publication or registration with certain goods/services on or in connection with which it has used the mark in commerce and retain an active application for any remaining goods/services, a divisional application and fee are required. 37 C.F.R. §2.87)

PTO Form 1581 (REV. 6-96)
OMB No. 0651-0009
Exp. (06/30/98)     There is no requirement to respond to this collection of information unless a currently valid OMB Number is displayed.

U.S. Department of Commerce/Patent and Trademark Office

# INSTRUCTIONS AND INFORMATION FOR APPLICANT

Applicant must file a Statement of Use within six months after the mailing of the Notice of Allowance based upon a bona fide intention to use a mark in commerce, UNLESS, within that same period, applicant submits a request for a six-month extension of time to file the Statement of Use. The written request **must**:

    (1)    be received in the PTO within six months after the issue date of the Notice of Allowance,

    (2)    include applicant's verified statement of continued bona fide intention to use the mark in commerce,

    (3)    specify the goods/services to which the request pertains as they are identified in the Notice of Allowance, and

    (4)    include a fee of $100 for each class of goods/services **(please note that fees are subject to change, usually on October 1 of each year).**

Applicant may request four further six-month extensions of time. No extensions may extend beyond 36 months from the issue date of the Notice of Allowance. Each further request must be received in the PTO within the previously granted six-month extension period and must include, in addition to the above requirements, a showing of **GOOD CAUSE**. This good cause showing must include:

    (1)    applicant's statement that the mark has not been used in commerce yet on all the goods or services specified in the Notice of Allowance with which applicant has a continued bona fide intention to use the mark in commerce, **and**

    (2)    applicant's statement of ongoing efforts to make such use, which may include the following: (a) product or service research or development, (b) market research, (c) promotional activities, (d) steps to acquire distributors, (e) steps to obtain required governmental approval, or (f) similar specified activity.

Applicant may submit one additional six-month extension request during the existing period in which applicant files the Statement of Use, unless the granting of this request would extend the period beyond 36 months from the issue date of the Notice of Allowance. As a showing of good cause for such a request, applicant should state its belief that applicant has made valid use of the mark in commerce, as evidenced by the submitted Statement of Use, but that if the Statement is found by the PTO to be defective, applicant will need additional time in which to file a new statement of use.

Only the following person may sign the declaration of the Request for Extension of Time: (a) the individual applicant; (b) an officer of corporate applicant: (c) one general partner of partnership applicant; (d) all joint applicants.

## MAILING INSTRUCTIONS

> MAIL COMPLETED FORM TO:
>
> **ASSISTANT COMMISSIONER FOR TRADEMARKS**
> **BOX ITU**
> **2900 CRYSTAL DRIVE**
> **ARLINGTON, VIRGINIA 22202-3513**

Please note that the filing date of a document in the Patent and Trademarks Office is the date of receipt in the Office, not the date of deposit of the mail. 37 C.F. R. §1.6. To avoid lateness due to mail delay, use of the certificate of mailing set forth below is encouraged.

## CERTIFICATE OF MAILING

I do hereby certify that this correspondence is being **deposited** with the United States Postal Service as first class mail, postage prepaid, in an envelope addressed to the Assistant Commissioner for Trademarks, 2900 Crystal Drive, Arlington, VA 22202-3513, on _____ (date).

_____

Signature

Date of Deposit

_____

Print or Type Name of Person Signing Certificate

This form is estimated to take 15 minutes to complete including time required for reading and understanding instructions, gathering necessary information, record keeping and actually providing the information. Any comments on the amount of time you require to complete this form should be sent to the Office of Management and Organization, U.S. Patent and Trademark Office, U.S. Department of Commerce, Washington, D.C. 20231. Do not send forms to this address.

TRADEMARK

# UNITED STATES DEPARTMENT OF COMMERCE
# PATENT AND TRADEMARK OFFICE

Applicant

Mark

Serial Number

Trademark Law Office _____

Trademark Attorney _____

Filed _____

Commissioner of Patents and Trademarks
Washington, D.C. 20231

## REQUEST TO DIVIDE APPLICATION

The applicant hereby requests that the application identified above be divided as follows:

Please retain in the original application the following goods/services—(use the language of the original application insofar as possible)

Please include in the new, divided application the following goods/services—(They should be different from and should not overlap, those remaining in the original application.)

(check one)

☐　　Enclosed is a check in payment of the filing fee for the divided application

☐　　The divided application includes all goods or services in a single class presented in the original, parent application; therefore the applicant submits that no filing fee is due or required.

DATED:

Respectfully,

_____

Telephone Number:
Address:

<table>
<tr>
<td rowspan="2">

**DECLARATION OF USE OF A MARK UNDER SECTION 8 OF THE TRADEMARK ACT OF 1946, AS AMENDED**

</td>
<td colspan="2">MARK (Identify the mark)</td>
</tr>
<tr>
<td>REGISTRATION NO.</td>
<td>DATE OF REGISTRATION:</td>
</tr>
</table>

**TO THE ASSISTANT SECRETARY AND COMMISSIONER OF PATENTS AND TRADEMARKS:**

REGISTRANT'S NAME:[1]

REGISTRANT'S CURRENT MAILING ADDRESS: _____

**GOODS AND/OR SERVICES AND USE IN COMMERCE STATEMENT:**

The mark shown in Registration No. _____ owned by the above-identified registrant is in use in

_____ commerce on or in connection with all of the goods and/or services identified in the
 (type of)[2]

registration, (*except* for the following)[3] _____

_____ ;

as evidenced by the attached specimen(s)[4] showing the mark as currently used.

**DECLARATION**

The undersigned being hereby warned that willful false statements and the like so made are punishable by fine or imprisonment, or both, under 18 U.S.C. 1001, and that such willful false statements may jeopardize the validity of this document, declares that he/she is properly authorized to execute this document on behalf of the registrant; he/she believes the registrant to be the owner of the above identified registration; the trademark/service mark is in use in commerce; and all statements made of his/her own knowledge are true and all statements made on information and belief are believed to be true.

_____
Date

_____
Signature

_____
Telephone Number

_____
Print or Type Name and Position
[if applicable][5]

## FOOTNOTES

1. The present owner of the registration must file this form between the 5th and 6th year after the date of registration. If ownership of the registration has changed since the registration date, provide supporting documentation if available or a verified explanation. The present owner should refer to itself as the registrant.

2. "Type of Commerce" must be specified as "interstate," "territorial," "foreign," or such other commerce as may lawfully be regulated by Congress. Foreign registrants must specify commerce which Congress may regulate, using wording such as "foreign commerce between the U.S. and a foreign country."

3. List only those goods and/or services for which registrant is no longer using the mark. You should fill in this blank **only** if you are no longer using the mark on all the goods or services in the registration.

4. A specimen showing current use of the registered mark for at least one product or service in each class of the registration must be submitted with this form. Examples of specimens are tags or labels for goods, and advertisements for services. The registration number should be printed directly on the specimen.

5. If the present owner is an individual, the individual should sign the declaration.

6. If the present owner is a partnership, the declaration should be signed by a General Partner.

7. If the present owner is a corporation or similar juristic entity, the declaration should be signed by an officer of the corporation/entity. Please print or type the officer title of the person signing the declaration.

NOTE: If the registration is owned by more than one party, as joint owners, each owner must sign this declaration.

## FEES

For each declaration under Section 8, the required fee is $100.00 per international class. Please be aware that our fees may change. Changes, if any, are normally effective October 1 of each year. If this declaration is intended to cover less than the total number of classes in the registration, please specify the classes for which the declaration is submitted. The declaration, with appropriate fee(s), should be sent to:

**BOX POST REG**
**FEE**
**Assistant Commissioner for Trademarks**
**2900 Crystal Drive**
**Arlington, Virginia 22202-3513**

## PTO Notification

You should receive written notification from the PTO of either the acceptance or rejection of this post registration document. If you do not receive written notification from the PTO within six months after filing, you may wish to telephone the Trademark Status Line at (703) 305-8747 or the Post Registration Division at (703) 308-9500.

## MAILING INSTRUCTION BOX

*You can ensure timely filing of this form by following the procedure described in 37 CFR 1.10 as follows: (1) on or before the due date for filing this form, deposit the completed form with the U.S. Post Office using the "Express Mail Post Office to Addressee" Service; (2) include a certificate of "Express Mail" under 37 CFR 1.10. Papers properly mailed under 37 CFR 1.10 are considered received by the PTO on the date that they are deposited with the Post Office.*

When placing the certificate directly on the correspondence, use the following language:

**Certificate of Express Mail Under 37 CFR 1.10**

"Express Mail" mailing label number: _____
Date of Deposit: _____
I hereby certify that this paper and fee is being deposited with the United States Postal Service "Express Mail Post Office to Addressee" service under 37 CFR 1.10 on the date indicated above and is addressed to the Assistant Commissioner for Trademarks, 2900 Crystal Drive, Arlington, Virginia 22202-3513.

_____     _____
(Typed or printed name of person mailing paper & fee)          (Signature of person mailing paper & fee)

| DECLARATION OF INCONTESTABILITY OF A MARK UNDER **SECTION 15** OF THE TRADEMARK ACT OF 1946 AS AMENDED | MARK (Identify the mark) | |
|---|---|---|
| | REGISTRATION NO. | DATE OF REGISTRATION: |

## TO THE ASSISTANT SECRETARY AND COMMISSIONER OF PATENTS AND TRADEMARKS:

REGISTRANT'S NAME:[1]

REGISTRANT'S CURRENT MAILING ADDRESS: _____

_____

_____

GOODS AND/OR SERVICES AND USE IN COMMERCE STATEMENT:

The mark shown in **Principal Register** Registration No._____, owned by the above-identified

registrant has been incontinuous use in _____ commerce for five consecutive years from _____
                                                    (type of)[2]                                                                                        (date)

to the present on or in connection with all of the goods and/or services identified in the registration, (*except* for the following)[3]

_____

_____.

There has been no final decision adverse to registrant's claim of ownership of such mark for such goods or

services, or to registrant's right to register the same or to keep the same on the register; and there is no

proceeding involving said rights pending and not disposed of either in the Patent and Trademark Office or in

the courts.

### DECLARATION

The undersigned being hereby warned that willful false statements and the like so made are punishable by fine or imprisonment, or both, under 18 U.S.C. 1001, and that such willful false statements may jeopardize the validity of this document, declares that he/she is properly authorized to execute this document on behalf of the registrant; he/she believes the registrant to be the owner of the above identified registration; the trademark/service mark is in use in commerce; and all statements made of his/her own knowledge are true and all statements made on information and belief are believed to be true.

_____            _____
Date                                                          Signature

_____            _____
Telephone Number                                    Print or Type Name and Position
                                                                   [if applicable][4]

## FOOTNOTES

1. The present owner of the Principal Register registration must file this form. If ownership of the registration has changed since the registration date, provide supporting documentation if available or a verified explanation. If the present owner is a successor to the original registrant, then the present owner should refer to itself as the registrant. **Please note that Section 15 is only applicable to Principal Register registrations.**

2. "Type of Commerce" must be specified as "interstate," "territorial," "foreign," or such other commerce as may lawfully be regulated by Congress. Foreign registrants must specify commerce which Congress may regulate, using wording such as "foreign commerce between the U.S. and a foreign country."

3. List only those goods and/or services for which registrant is no longer using the mark. You should fill in this blank **only** if you are no longer using the mark on all the goods or services in the registration.

4. If the present owner is an individual, the individual should sign the declaration.

5. If the present owner is a partnership, the declaration should be signed by a General Partner.

6. If the present owner is a corporation or similar juristic entity, the declaration should be signed by an officer of the corporation/entity. Please print or type the officer title of the person signing the declaration.

NOTE: If the registration is owned by more than one party, as joint owners, each owner must sign this declaration.

## FEES

For each declaration under Section 15, the required fee is $100.00 per international class. Please be aware that our fees may change. Changes, if any, are normally effective October 1 of each year. If this declaration is intended to cover less than the total number of classes in the registration, please specify the classes for which the declaration is submitted. The declaration, with appropriate fee(s), should be sent to:

**BOX POST REG**
**FEE**
**Assistant Commissioner for Trademarks**
**2900 Crystal Drive**
**Arlington, Virginia 22202-3513**

## PTO Notification

You should receive written notification from the PTO of either the acceptance or rejection of this post registration document. If you do not receive written notification from the PTO within six months after filing, you may wish to telephone the Trademark Status Line at (703) 305-8747 or the Post Registration Division at (703) 308-9500.

## MAILING INSTRUCTION BOX

*You can ensure timely filing of this form by following the procedure described in 37 CFR 1.10 as follows: (1) on or before the due date for filing this form, deposit the completed form with the U.S. Post Office using the "Express Mail Post Office to Addressee" Service; (2) include a certificate of "Express Mail" under 37 CFR 1.10.* Papers properly mailed under 37 CFR 1.10 are considered received by the PTO on the date that they are deposited with the Post Office.

When placing the certificate directly on the correspondence, use the following language:

**Certificate of Express Mail Under 37 CFR 1.10**

"Express Mail" mailing label number: ————————————————
Date of Deposit: _____
I hereby certify that this paper and fee is being deposited with the United States Postal Service "Express Mail Post Office to Addressee" service under 37 CFR 1.10 on the date indicated above and is addressed to the Assistant Commissioner for Trademarks, 2900 Crystal Drive, Arlington, Virginia 22202-3513.

_____          _____
(Typed or printed name of person mailing paper & fee)          (Signature of person mailing paper & fee)

This form is estimated to take 15 minutes to complete. Time will vary depending upon the needs of the individual case. Any comments on the amount of time you require to complete this form should be sent to the Office of Management and Organization, U.S. Patent and Trademark Office, U.S. Department of Commerce, Washington, D.C. 20231, and to the Office of Information and Regulatory Affairs, Office of Management and Budget, Washington, D.C. 20503. **DO NOT SEND FORMS TO EITHER OF THESE ADDRESS.**

| COMBINED DECLARATION OF USE AND INCONTESTABILITY UNDER **SECTIONS 8 & 15**[1] OF THE TRADEMARK ACT OF 1946, AS AMENDED | MARK (Identify the mark) | |
|---|---|---|
| | REGISTRATION NO. | DATE OF REGISTRATION: |

**TO THE ASSISTANT SECRETARY AND COMMISSIONER OF PATENTS AND TRADEMARKS:**

REGISTRANT'S NAME:[2]

REGISTRANT'S CURRENT MAILING ADDRESS  _____
_____
_____

GOODS AND/OR SERVICES AND USE IN COMMERCE STATEMENT:

The mark shown in Registration No. _____, owned by the above-identified registrant, has been in

continuous use in _____ commerce for five consecutive years from the date of registration or the
(type of)[3]

date of publication under §12(c)[4] to the present, on or in connection with all the goods and/or services

identified in the registration, (*except* for the following)[5] _____

_____ ;

as evidenced by the attached specimen(s)[6] showing the mark as currently used. There has been no final

decision adverse to registrant's claim of ownership of such mark for such goods or services, or to registrant's

right to register the same or to keep the same on the register; and there is no proceeding involving said

rights pending and not disposed of either in the Patent and Trademark Office or in the courts.

## DECLARATION

The undersigned being hereby warned that willful false statements and the like so made are punishable by fine or imprisonment, or both, under 18 U.S.C. 1001, and that such willful false statements may jeopardize the validity of this document, declares that he/she is properly authorized to execute this document on behalf of the registrant; he/she believes the registrant to be the owner of the above identified registration; the trademark/service mark is in use in commerce; and all statements made of his/her own knowledge are true and all statements made on information and belief are believed to be true.

_____          _____
Date                                                              Signature

_____          _____
Telephone Number                                         Print or Type Name and Position
                                                                      [if applicable][5]

PTO-FB-TM (Combined 8 & 15) (Rev. 1/93)          U.S. DEPARTMENT OF COMMERCE/Patent and Trademark Office
OMB No. 0651-0009

## FOOTNOTES

1. If you do not have five years of **continuous** use, you should file a Section 8 affidavit only. Please see PTO Form#1583.

2. The present owner of the registration must file this form between the 5th and 6th year after registration. If ownership of the registration has changed since the registration date, provide supporting documentation if available or a verified explanation. The present owner should refer to itself as the registrant.

3. "Type of Commerce" must be specified as "interstate," "territorial," "foreign," or such other commerce as may lawfully be regulated by Congress. Foreign registrants must specify commerce which Congress may regulate, using wording such as "foreign commerce between the U.S. and a foreign country."

4. This combined form is only appropriate when the five year period of continuous use, which is required for Section 15, (1) occurs between the 5th and 6th year after registration, or (2) after publication under §12(c) as is required for Section 8.

5. List only those goods and/or services for which registrant is no longer using the mark. You should fill in this blank **only** if you are no longer using the mark on all the goods or services in the registration.

6. A specimen showing current use of the registered mark for at least one product or service in each class of the registration must be submitted with this form. Examples of specimens are tags or labels for goods, and advertisements for services.

7. If the present owner is an individual, the individual should sign the declaration.

   If the present owner is a partnership, the declaration should be signed by a General Partner.

   If the present owner is a corporation or similar juristic entity, the declaration should be signed by an officer of the corporation/entity. Please print or type the officer title of the person signing the declaration.

NOTE: If the registration is owned by more than one party, as joint owners, each owner must sign this declaration.

## PTO Notification

You should receive written notification from the PTO of either the acceptance or rejection of this post registration document. If you do not receive written notification from the PTO within six months after filing, you may wish to telephone the Trademark Status Line at (703) 305-8747 or the Post Registration Division at (703) 308-9500

## FEES

For each declaration under Sections 8 & 15, the required fee is $200.00 per international class. Please be aware that our fees may change. Changes, if any, are normally effective October 1 of each year. If this declaration is intended to cover less than the total number of classes in the registration, please specify the classes for which the declaration is submitted. The declaration, with appropriate fee(s), should be sent to:

BOX POST REG
FEE
Assistant Commissioner for Trademarks
2900 Crystal Drive
Arlington, Virginia 22202-3513

## MAILING INSTRUCTION BOX

*You can ensure timely filing of this form by following the procedure described in 37 CFR 1.10 as follows: (1) on or before the due date for filing this form, deposit the completed form with the U.S. Post Office using the "Express Mail Post Office to Addressee" Service; (2) include a certificate of "Express Mail" under 37 CFR 1.10.* Papers properly mailed under 37 CFR 1.10 are considered received by the PTO on the date that they are deposited with the Post Office.

When placing the certificate directly on the correspondence, use the following language:

**Certificate of Express Mail Under 37 CFR 1.10**

"Express Mail" mailing label number: _____
Date of Deposit: _____
I hereby certify that this paper and fee is being deposited with the United States Postal Service "Express Mail Post Office to Addressee" service under 37 CFR 1.10 on the date indicated above and is addressed to the Commissioner of Patents and Trademarks, Washington, D.C. 20231.

_____          _____
(Typed or printed name of person mailing paper & fee)          (Signature of person mailing paper & fee)

This form is estimated to take 15 minutes to complete. Time will vary depending upon the needs of the individual case. Any comments on the amount of time you require to complete this form should be sent to the Office of Management and Organization, U.S. Patent and Trademark Office, U.S. Department of Commerce, Washington, D.C. 20231, and to the Office of Information and Regulatory Affairs, Office of Management and Budget, Washington, D.C. 20503. **DO NOT SEND FORMS TO EITHER OF THESE ADDRESSES.**

<table>
<tr><td rowspan="3">

**APPLICATION FOR RENEWAL OF REGISTRATION OF A MARK UNDER SECTION 9 OF THE TRADEMARK ACT OF 1946, AS AMENDED**

</td><td colspan="2">MARK (Identify the mark)</td></tr>
<tr><td>REGISTRATION NO.</td><td>DATE OF REGISTRATION:</td></tr>
</table>

**TO THE ASSISTANT SECRETARY AND COMMISSIONER OF PATENTS AND TRADEMARKS:**

REGISTRANT'S NAME:[1]

REGISTRANT'S CURRENT MAILING ADDRESS: _____

_____

_____

**GOODS AND/OR SERVICES AND USE IN COMMERCE STATEMENT:**

The mark shown in Registration No. _____ owned by the above-identified registrant is still in use in

_____ commerce on or in connection with all of the goods and/or services identified in the

(type of)[2]

registration, (*except* for the following)[3] _____

_____

as evidenced by the attached specimen(s)[4] showing the mark as currently used.

## DECLARATION

The undersigned being hereby warned that willful false statements and the like so made are punishable by fine or imprisonment, or both, under 18 U.S.C. 1001, and that such willful false statements may jeopardize the validity of this document, declares that he/she is properly authorized to execute this document on behalf of the registrant; he/she believes the registrant to be the owner of the above identified registration; the trademark/service mark is in use in commerce; and all statements made of his/her own knowledge are true and all statements made on information and belief are believed to be true.

_____                    _____
Date                                         Signature

_____                    _____
Telephone Number                             Print or Type Name and Position
                                             [if applicable][5]

## FOOTNOTES

1. The present owner of the registration must file this form within 6 months prior to the expiration of the registration term. The form may also be filed within a 3 month grace period following the expiration of the registration term upon payment of the late fee. If ownership of the registration has changed since the registration date, provide supporting documentation if available or a verified explanation. The present owner should refer to itself as the registrant.

2. "Type of Commerce" must be specified as "interstate," "territorial," "foreign," or such other commerce as may lawfully be regulated by Congress. Foreign registrants must specify commerce which Congress may regulate, using wording such as "foreign commerce between the U.S. and a foreign country."

3. List only those goods and/or services for which registrant is no longer using the mark. You should fill in this blank only if you are no longer using the mark on all the goods or services in the registration.

4. A specimen showing current use of the registered mark for at least one product or service in each class of the registration must be submitted with this form. Examples of specimens are tags or labels for goods, and advertisements for services. The registration number should be printed directly on the specimen.

5. If the present owner is an individual, the individual should sign the declaration.

6. If the present owner is a partnership, the declaration should be signed by a General Partner.

7. If the present owner is a corporation or similar juristic entity, the declaration should be signed by an officer of the corporation/entity. Please print or type the officer title of the person signing the declaration.

NOTE: If the registration is owned by more than one party, as joint owners, each owner must sign this declaration.

## PTO Notification

You should receive written notification from the PTO of either the acceptance or rejection of this post registration document. If you do not receive written notification from the PTO within six months after filing, you may wish to telephone the Trademark Status Line at (703) 305-8747 or the Post Registration Division at (703) 308-9500.

## FEES

For each renewal application under Section 9, the required fee is $300.00 per class. Please be aware that our fees may change. Changes, if any, are normally effective October 1 of each year. If filed during the three month grace period a late fee of $100.00 per class must also be submitted. If this renewal application is intended to cover less than the total number of classes in the registration, please specify the classes for which the renewal application is submitted. The renewal application, with appropriate fee(s), should be sent to:

**BOX POST REG**
**FEE**
**Assistant Commissioner for Trademarks**
**2900 Crystal Drive**
**Arlington, Virginia 22202-3513**

## MAILING INSTRUCTION BOX

*You can ensure timely filing of this form by following the procedure described in 37 CFR 1.10 as follows: (1) on or before the due date for filing this form, deposit the completed form with the U.S. Post Office using the "Express Mail Post Office to Addressee" Service; (2) include a certificate of "Express Mail" under 37 CFR 1.10.* Papers properly mailed under 37 CFR 1.10 are considered received by the PTO on the date that they are deposited with the Post Office.

When placing the certificate directly on the correspondence, use the following language:

**Certificate of Express Mail Under 37 CFR 1.10**

"Express Mail" mailing label number: _____

Date of Deposit: _____

I hereby certify that this paper and fee is being deposited with the United States Postal Service "Express Mail Post Office to Addressee" service under 37 CFR 1.10 on the date indicated above and is addressed to the Assistant Commissioner for Trademarks, 2900 Crystal Drive, Arlington, Virginia 22202-3513.

_____          _____
(Typed or printed name of person mailing paper & fee)          (Signature of person mailing paper & fee)

This form is estimated to take 15 minutes to complete. Time will vary depending upon the needs of the individual case. Any comments on the amount of time you require to complete this form should be sent to the Office of Management and Organization, U.S. Patent and Trademark Office, U.S. Department of Commerce, Washington, D.C. 20231, and to the Office of Information and Regulatory Affairs, Office of Management and Budget, Washington, D.C. 20503. **DO NOT SEND FORMS TO EITHER OF THESE ADDRESSES.**

| DESIGNATION OF DOMESTIC REPRESENTATIVE | MARK *(identify the mark)* |
|---|---|
| | REGISTRATION NO. (IF KNOWN) |
| | CLASS NO. (S) |

_____

*(name of domestic representative)*

whose postal address is _____

_____ is hereby designated applicant's representative upon whom

notice or process in proceedings affecting the mark may be served.


_____

*(signature of applicant or owner of mark)*


_____

*(date)*

| | |
|---|---|
| **ASSIGNMENT OF REGISTRATION OF A MARK** | MARK *(identify the mark)* |
| | REGISTRATION NO. (IF KNOWN) |
| | CLASS NO. (S) |

Whereas_____
*(name of assignor)*

whose postal address is _____

_____ has adopted, used and is using a mark which is registered in the

United States Patent and Trademark Office, Registration No. _____ dated

_____; and whereas _____
*(name of assignee)*

whose postal address is _____

is desirous of acquiring said mark and the registration thereof;

Now, therefore, for good and valuable consideration, receipt of which is hereby acknowledged, said

_____ does hereby assign unto the said
*(name of assignor)*

_____ all right, title and interest in and to
*(name of assignee)*

the said mark, together with the good will of the business symbolized by the mark, and the above registration

thereof.




_____

*(signature of assignor, if assignor is a corporation or other juristic organization give the official title of the person who signs for assignor)*


State of _____ ⎫
County of _____ ⎬ ss.
⎭

  On this _____ day of _____, 19____, before me appeared _____

_____ the person who signed this instrument, who acknowledged that he/she

signed it as a free act on his/her own behalf (or on behalf of the identified corporation or other juristic entity

with authority to do so).*



_____

*(signature of notary public)*


* The wording of the acknowledgment may vary in some jurisdictions. Be sure to use wording acceptable in the jurisdiction where the document is executed.

FORM PTO-1618A
Expires 06/30/99
OMB 0651-0027

U.S. Department of Commerce
Patent and Trademark Office
**TRADEMARK**

# RECORDATION FORM COVER SHEET
## TRADEMARKS ONLY

TO:  The Commissioner of Patents and Trademarks:  Please record the attached original document(s) or copy(ies).

## Submission Type

☐ **New**

☐ **Resubmission** **(Non-Recordation)**
Document ID # _____

☐ **Correction of PTO Error**
Reel # _____ Frame # _____

☐ **Corrective Document**
Reel # _____ Frame # _____

## Conveyance Type

☐ **Assignment**          ☐ **License**

☐ **Security Agreement**   ☐ **Nunc Pro Tunc Assignment**

☐ **Merger**          **Effective Date**
                      **Month  Day  Year**
                      _____

☐ **Change of Name**

☐ **Other** _____

## Conveying Party

☐ Mark if additional names of conveying parties attached          **Execution Date**
                                                                   **Month  Day  Year**

**Name** _____          _____

**Formerly** _____

☐ **Individual**   ☐ **General Partnership**   ☐ **Limited Partnership**   ☐ **Corporation**   ☐ **Association**

☐ **Other** _____

☐ **Citizenship/State of Incorporation/Organization** _____

## Receiving Party

☐ Mark if additional names of receiving parties attached

**Name** _____

**DBA/AKA/TA** _____

**Composed of** _____

**Address** (line 1) _____

**Address** (line 2) _____

**Address** (line 3) _____
City          State/Country          Zip Code

☐ **Individual**   ☐ **General Partnership**   ☐ **Limited Partnership**   ☐ If document to be recorded is an assignment and the receiving party is not domiciled in the United States, an appointment of a domestic representative should be attached.
*(Designation must be a separate document from Assignment.)*

☐ **Corporation**   ☐ **Association**

☐ **Other** _____

☐ **Citizenship/State of Incorporation/Organization** _____

## FOR OFFICE USE ONLY

Public burden reporting for this collection of information is estimated to average approximately 30 minutes per Cover Sheet to be recorded, including time for reviewing the document and gathering the data needed to complete the Cover Sheet.  Send comments regarding this burden estimate to the U.S. Patent and Trademark Office, Chief Information Officer,  Washington, D.C. 20231 and to the Office of Information and Regulatory Affairs, Office of Management and Budget, Paperwork Reduction Project (0651-0027), Washington, D.C. 20503.  See OMB Information Collection Budget Package  0651-0027, Patent and Trademark Assignment Practice.  DO NOT SEND REQUESTS TO RECORD ASSIGNMENT DOCUMENTS TO THIS ADDRESS.

**Mail documents to be recorded with required cover sheet(s) information to:**
**Commissioner of Patents and Trademarks, Box Assignments , Washington, D.C. 20231**

FORM PTO-1618B
Expires 06/30/99
OMB 0651-0027

**Page 2**

U.S. Department of Commerce
Patent and Trademark Office
**TRADEMARK**

## Domestic Representative Name and Address

Enter for the first Receiving Party only.

**Name**

**Address (line 1)**

**Address (line 2)**

**Address (line 3)**

**Address (line 4)**

## Correspondent Name and Address

Area Code and Telephone Number

**Name**

**Address (line 1)**

**Address (line 2)**

**Address (line 3)**

**Address (line 4)**

## Pages

Enter the total number of pages of the attached conveyance document including any attachments.

\#

## Trademark Application Number(s) or Registration Number(s)

☐ Mark if additional numbers attached

*Enter either the Trademark Application Number or the Registration Number (DO NOT ENTER BOTH numbers for the same property).*

| Trademark Application Number(s) | | | Registration Number(s) | | |
|---|---|---|---|---|---|
| | | | | | |
| | | | | | |
| | | | | | |

## Number of Properties

Enter the total number of properties involved.     \#

## Fee Amount

Fee Amount for Properties Listed (37 CFR 3.41):     $

**Method of Payment:**     Enclosed ☐     Deposit Account ☐

**Deposit Account**

*(Enter for payment by deposit account or if additional fees can be charged to the account.)*

**Deposit Account Number:**     \#

Authorization to charge additional fees:     Yes ☐     No ☐

## Statement and Signature

*To the best of my knowledge and belief, the foregoing information is true and correct and any attached copy is a true copy of the original document. Charges to deposit account are authorized, as indicated herein.*

_____     _____     _____
**Name of Person Signing**               **Signature**                    **Date Signed**

# GUIDELINES FOR COMPLETING TRADEMARK RECORDATION COVER SHEET

A cover sheet and any necessary continuation sheets must be submitted with each document to be recorded. Information required for recordation will be extracted from the cover sheets and cover sheet continuation forms only. The submitted cover sheets will become part of the public record. If the document to be recorded concerns both patents and trademarks, a separate patent and a separate trademark cover sheet, including any attached continuing information, must accompany the document. If the document concerns multiple conveyances or transfers, a cover sheet must be submitted for each. Enter all required information using standard business block-style print (e.g. Courier 10 pitch) Each line allows up to 40 characters including spaces. This information must be submitted on the USPTO provided form. NO PHOTOCOPIES of the USPTO Recordation Form Cover Sheet or Recordation Form Cover Sheet Continuation will be accepted. The USPTO provided cover sheets are printed in drop out ink form. Completed cover sheets will be scanned for image capture and Optical Character Recognition (OCR) processing to extract the recordation data. For assistance in completing this cover sheet, obtaining additional cover sheets, and information, call (703) 308-9723.

Submission Type - Each submission type requires a new cover sheet. Enter an "X" in the appropriate box indicating the type of submission. If the conveyance document is being submitted for recordation for the first time, enter an " X" in the box for New Assignment. If the submission is a Non-recordation, enter an "X" for Re-submission and provide the document identification number of the original submission. Resubmitted non-recordation documents require a new cover sheet (the new cover sheet shall contain all of the appropriate data and the fee required for recordation). If a previously recorded document requires correction due to a data entry error, enter an "X" for Public Correction and provide the reel and frame number of the original document. Requests to correct the data entry error must be submitted on a new cover sheet. The cover sheet shall contain only the data element in question, the name, date and signature of the person submitting the request, and any other pertinent information, (enter the correspondent's name and address, if it has changed since the document was recorded). If a previously recorded document was submitted with erroneous information, enter an "X" indicating Corrective Assignment and provide the reel and frame number of the previously recorded document. A Corrective Assignment requires a new cover sheet as provided in 37CFR 1.334. If the submission type is not listed, enter an "X" in the Other box and specify the submission type.

Conveyance Type - Enter an "X" in the appropriate box describing the nature of the conveying document. If the document is a nunc pro tunc assignment, enter the effective date using the numerical representation of the date without slashes (/) formatted as MMDDYYYY (05141993). If the conveyance type is not listed, enter an "X" in Other Box and specify the nature of the conveyance .

Conveying Party - Enter the full names of all party(ies) conveying the interest. If the conveying party is an individual, enter the last name first, followed by the first name followed by the middle initial. Separate the last and first name by a comma followed by a blank space. For example, "Carter, Constance M." Separate the last and first name by a comma, followed by a blank space. If the conveying party is a corporation and the corporation name begins with "The", the name must be entered as Longmire Cookie Company, The. A Formerly statement. must be entered by placing the word "Formerly " in front of the former business name, separated by a comma (this data is optional). Enter the execution date of the document (i.e. the date the document is signed by each conveying party) using the numerical representation of the month, day, and year without slashes (/) formatted as MMDDYYYY (05141993). Do not use the European date style when entering the date. Indicate the entity and citizenship of each conveying party. If the conveying party is an individual, the country of citizenship must be indicated. If the conveying party is not an individual, then, if it is a U.S. entity, the state under whose laws it is organized should be set out, if it is a foreign entity, the country under whose laws it is organized should be set out. Thus, a U.S. corporation would indicate its state of incorporation, while a foreign corporation would indicate its country of incorporation. The names, execution dates entity and citizenship of additional conveying parties must be entered on the formatted Recordation Form Cover Sheet Continuation. If the entity type is not listed, enter an "X" in the Other Box and specify the entity type. If there are additional conveying parties, enter an "X" in the box indicating additional conveying information is attached. Only the names appearing on the cover sheet and continuation sheets will be recorded.

Receiving Party. - Enter the full name and address of the party(ies) receiving an interest in. If the receiving party is an individual, enter last name first, followed by the first name, followed by the middle initial. Separate the last and first name by a comma, followed by a blank space. If the receiving party is a corporation and the corporation name begins with "The", the name must be entered as" Longmire Cookie Company, The." Indicate the names, and entity of each receiving party. Enter optional information regarding either DBA/AKA/TA , or Composed of, as appropriate. DBA means Doing Business As; AKA means Also Known As; and TA means

Trading As. Enter the appropriate acronym (i.e. DBA, AKA, TA, or Composed of ) in front of the business name, separated by a comma. For example, Longmire Cookie Company, The, DBA, Longmire Cookies (this data is optional). Enter up to three lines of address: address line 1 is used to enter the street address; address line 2 is used to enter the floor/room number, suite number or department location; and address line 3 is used to enter the City, State, and zip code. Use the two letter state code when entering the state, (i.e. VA for the state of Virginia). Only the names which appear on this cover sheet and the Recordation Cover Sheet Continuation form(s) will be recorded.

Indicate the entity and citizenship of each receiving party. If the receiving party is an individual, the country of citizenship must be indicated. If the receiving party is not an individual, then, if it is a U.S. entity, the state under whose laws it is organized should be set out, if it is a foreign entity, the country under whose laws it is organized should be set out. Thus a U.S. corporation would indicate its state of incorporation, while a foreign corporation would indicate its country of incorporation (this data is optional). If the document to be recorded is an assignment and the receiving party is not domiciled in the United States, an appointment of domestic representative should be attached. A designation of domestic representative must be contained in a document separate from the assignment document. Enter an "X" in the box to indicate that a designation of domestic representative is attached. If there is more than one party receiving an interest in the property, enter an "X" in the box to indicate that additional information is attached. Only the names which appear on this cover sheet and the Recordation Cover Sheet Continuation form(s) will be recorded.

Correspondent Name and Address - Enter the full name and address of the party to whom correspondence is to be mailed. Each line of address allows up to 40 characters including spaces. Address information will be used to create a mailing label in order to return the document to the submitter. Enter the telephone number and area code of the correspondent.

Number of Pages - Enter the total number of pages contained in the conveyance document, including any attachments. If the document to be recorded concerns both patents and trademarks, separate patent and trademark cover sheets must accompany the document. Do not include the Recordation Form Cover Sheet pages in this total.

Application Numbers or Registration Numbers - Enter the trademark application number(s) (an eight (8) digit number consisting of a two (2) digit series code and a six (6) digit serial number) against which the document is to be recorded. Enter application number(s) as 74105889). (Do not enter a slash, space or comma between the series code and the serial number). If an application has matured into a trademark registration, enter the seven digit trademark registration number(s) against which the document is to be recorded. Enter registration numbers as 1714456. Do not enter both the application number and the registration number for the same property. Enter application numbers in the space designed for application number(s) and enter registration number(s) in the designated space. Enter property numbers in the designated boxes. Enter an "X" in the appropriate box indicating additional numbers are attached. Enter additional numbers on the Recordation Form Cover Sheet Continuation.

Number of Properties - Enter the total number of applications and registrations identified for recordation including properties indicated on any attached formatted Recordation Form Cover Sheet Continuation(s). Total Fee Enclosed and Deposit Account Number - A fee is required for each application and patent property against which the document is to be recorded. If the submission concerns multiple conveyances or transfers, a fee must be submitted separately for each property of each conveyance or transfer. Enter the Fee Amount calculated per cover sheet. Enter the Total Fee Enclosed, if payment is made by other than deposit account. If payment is by deposit account, enter the total amount authorized to be charged to the deposit account or merely the "amount due." Enter the deposit account number for authorized charges. Enter an "X" in the Yes or No box indicating authorization to "charge additional fees" to the deposit account. If additional fees are required, the USPTO will generate a request to the USPTO Office of Finance to charge additional fees to the deposit account. A copy of this request will be returned to the submitter with the Notice of Recordation .

Statement and Signature - Enter the name of the person submitting the document. The submitter must sign and date the cover sheet, confirming that to the best of the person's knowledge and belief, the information contained on the cover sheet is correct and that any copy of the document is a true copy of the original document and authorized charges to Deposit Account. The signature and date must appear to the right of the typed name. The document may be signed by the person whose name appears on the documents to be recorded: In the case of an individual, the individual's signature, for a corporation, the signature of an officer, for a partnership, the signature of a general partner, or in any case, the attorney representing such person or entity may sign the document.

# RECORDATION FORM COVER SHEET
## CONTINUATION
## TRADEMARKS ONLY

FORM PTO-1618C
Expires 06/30/99
OMB 0651-0027

U.S. Department of Commerce
Patent and Trademark Office
**TRADEMARK**

## Conveying Party
Enter Additional Conveying Party

☐ Mark if additional names of conveying parties attached

Execution Date
Month   Day   Year

**Name** _____

**Formerly** _____

☐ Individual   ☐ General Partnership   ☐ Limited Partnership   ☐ Corporation   ☐ Association

☐ Other _____

☐ Citizenship State of Incorporation/Organization _____

## Receiving Party
Enter Additional Receiving Party

☐ Mark if additional names of receiving parties attached

**Name** _____

**DBA/AKA/TA** _____

**Composed of** _____

**Address** (line 1) _____

**Address** (line 2) _____

**Address** (line 3) _____

City     State/Country     Zip Code

☐ Individual   ☐ General Partnership   ☐ Limited Partnership

☐ Corporation   ☐ Association

☐ Other _____

☐ If document to be recorded is an assignment and the receiving party is not domiciled in the United States, an appointment of a domestic representative should be attached *(Designation must be a separate document from the Assignment.)*

☐ Citizenship/State of Incorporation/Organization _____

## Trademark Application Number(s) or Registration Number(s)

☐ Mark if additional numbers attached

*Enter either the Trademark Application Number or the Registration Number (DO NOT ENTER BOTH numbers for the same property).*

### Trademark Application Number(s)

| | | |
|---|---|---|
| | | |
| | | |
| | | |
| | | |
| | | |
| | | |
| | | |

### Registration Number(s)

| | | |
|---|---|---|
| | | |
| | | |
| | | |
| | | |
| | | |
| | | |
| | | |

# GUIDELINES FOR COMPLETING TRADEMARK RECORDATION COVER SHEET CONTINUATION

Enter any additional information on the Recordation Form Cover Sheet Continuation. Use as many continuation sheets as necessary. Use the same guidelines as appropriate for the Item where the additional data will be entered.

Conveying Party - Enter the full names) of all party(ies) conveying the interest. If the conveying party(ies) is an individual, enter the last name followed by the first name and separated by a comma (i.e. Smith, John). If the conveying party is a corporation and the corporation name begins with "The", the name must be entered as Longmire Cookie Company, The. A Formerly statement. must be entered by placing the word "Formerly" in front of the former business name (this data is optional). Enter the execution date of the document (i.e. the date the document is signed by each conveying party. This date must be entered as the numerical representation of the date without slashes (/) formatted as MMDDYYYY (05141993). Do not use the European date style when entering the date. Indicate the entity and citizenship of each conveying party. If the conveying party is an individual, the country of citizenship must be indicated. If the conveying party is not an individual, then, if it is a U.S. entity, the state under whose laws it is organized should be set out, if it is a foreign entity, the country under whose laws it is organized should be set out. Thus, a U.S. corporation would indicate its state of incorporation, while a foreign corporation would indicate its country of incorporation. The names, execution dates entity and citizenship of additional conveying parties must be entered on the formatted Recordation Form Cover Sheet Continuation. If the entity type is not listed, enter an "X" in the Other Box and specify the entity type. If there are additional conveying parties, enter an "X" in the box indicating additional conveying information is attached. Only the names appearing on the cover sheet and continuation sheets will be recorded.

Receiving Party. - Enter the full name and address of the all parties) receiving an interest in the property. If the receiving party is an individual, enter the last name followed by the first name and separate by a comma (i.e. Smith, John). If the receiving party is a corporation and the corporation name begins with "The", the name must be entered as" Longmire Cookie Company, The." Indicate the names, and entity of each receiving party as well as the execution dates) of the document. Enter optional information regarding either DBA/AKA/TA, or Composed of, as appropriate. DBA means Doing Business As; AKA means Also Known As; and TA means Trading As. Enter the appropriate acronym (i.e. DBA, AKA, TA, or Composed of ) in front of the business name. For example, Longmire Cookie Company, The, DBA Longmire Cookies. This data is optional. Enter up to three lines of address: address line 1 is used to enter the floor/room number, suite number or department location; address line 2 is used to enter the street address; and address line 3 is used to enter the City, State, and zip code. Use the two letter state code when entering the state, (i.e. VA for the state of Virginia).

Indicate the entity and citizenship of each receiving party. If the receiving party is an individual, the country of citizenship must be indicated. If the receiving party is not an individual, then, if it is a U.S. entity, the state under whose laws it is organized should be set out, if it is a foreign entity, the country under whose laws it is organized should be set out. Thus a U.S. corporation would indicate its state of incorporation, while a foreign corporation would indicate its country of incorporation. If the document to be recorded is an assignment and the receiving party is not domiciled in the United States, an appointment of domestic representative should be attached. A designation of domestic representative must be contained in a document separate from the assignment document. Enter an "X" in the box to indicate that a designation of domestic representative is attached. If there is more than one party receiving an interest in the property, enter an "X" in the box to indicate that additional information is attached. Only the names appearing on the cover sheet and continuation sheets will be recorded.

Application Numbers or Registration Numbers - Enter the trademark application number (an eight (8) digit number consisting of a two (2) digit series code and a six (6) digit serial number. Enter trademark application numbers as 74105889. ( Do not enter a slash, space or comma between the series code and the serial number). or trademark registration number (a seven (7) digit number) against which the document is to be recorded. Enter application numbers in the space designed for application number and enter registration numbers in the designated space. If an application has matured into a trademark registration , enter only the registration number. Do not enter both the application number and the registration number for the same property. Enter property numbers in the designated boxes (i.e. 1714456 1654123 1682147). Enter an "X" in the appropriate box indicating additional numbers are attached. Enter additional numbers on the Recordation Form Cover Sheet Continuation.

Application to Record Trademark
with the United States Customs Service

To:    Intellectual Property Rights Branch
U. S. Customs Service
1301 Constitution Ave., N.W.
Washington, DC 20229

Name of trademark owner:

Address of trademark owner:

Trademark owner is:
❏   an individual who is a citizen of _____
❏   a partnership whose partners are citizens of _____
❏   an association or corporation which was organized under the laws of

_____

Places of manufacture of goods bearing the trademark:

The following are foreign persons authorized to use the trademark:

Name: Address:                            Use authorized:

Identification of any foreign parent or subsidiaries under common ownership or control which uses the trademark abroad*:

Include with this form:
1. A status copy of the certificate of registration certified by the U. S. Patent and Trademark Office showing title to be presently in the name of the applicant.
2. Five copies of the certificate or of a U. S. Patent and Trademark Office Certificate.
3. A fee of $190 for each class of goods sought to be protected.

*Note, "common ownership" means individual or aggregate ownership of more than 50% of the business entity and "common control" means effective control in policy and operations and is not necessarily synonymous with common ownership.

# BIBLIOGRAPHY

Hawes, James E. *Trademark Registration Practice*. New York: Clark Boardman Callaghan, 1987.

Kane, Siegrund D. *Trademark Law, A Practitioner's Guide*. New York: Practicing Law Institute, 1987.

Kilpatrick, Richard. *Likelihood of Confusion in Trademark Law*. New York: Practicing Law Institute, 1996.

Kramer, Barry and Allen D. Brufsky. *Trademark Law Practice Forms: Rules/Annotations/Commentary*. New York: Clark Boardman Co., Ltd., 1988.

McCarthy, J. Thomas. McCarthy on Trademark and Unfair Competition. New York: Clark Boardman Callaghan, 1996

Vandenburgh, Edward C. *Trademark Law and Practice*. 2d ed. Indianapolis: Bobbs-Merrill Co., Inc., 1968.

U.S. Department of Commerce. *Patent and Trademark Office. Trademark Manual of Examining Procedure*. 3d ed., 1997.

Trademark Act of 1946. 15 USC §1051 et seq.

Trademark Rules of Practice. 37 CFR §2.1 et seq.

# INDEX

*Your #1 Source for Real World Legal Information...*

# LEGAL SURVIVAL GUIDES™

- Written by lawyers
- Simple English explanation of the law
- Forms and instructions included

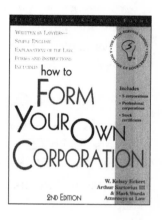

### HOW TO REGISTER YOUR OWN COPYRIGHT (2ND EDITION)

All of the information and forms needed to copyright any type of creative work, or how to use the works of others, is contained in this book. Learn to protect written, musical, audiovisual, and three dimensional works, as well as computer programs and designs.

160 pages; $19.95;
ISBN 1-57071-225-5

### LEGAL RESEARCH MADE EASY

This book for non-lawyers explains how to use the various types of legal reference books such as legal encyclopedias, statutes, digests, American Law Reports, and Shepard's Citations, as well as computerized legal databases. Includes state and federal materials.

124 pages; $14.95;
ISBN 1-57248-008-4

### HOW TO FORM YOUR OWN CORPORATION (2ND EDITION)

New business owners can save precious capital by forming their own corporations without the expense of a lawyer. This book includes a summary of the law and forms and instructions for forming a corporation in all 50 states and the District of Columbia.

180 pages; $19.95;
ISBN 1-57071-227-1

*What our customers say about our books:*

"It couldn't be more clear for the lay person." —R.D.

"I want you to know I really appreciate your book. It has saved me a lot of time and money." —L.T.

"Your real estate contracts book has saved me nearly $12,000.00 in closing costs over the past year." —A.B.

"...many of the legal questions that I have had over the years were answered clearly and concisely through your plain English interpretation of the law." —C.E.H.

"If there weren't people out there like you I'd be lost. You have the best books of this type out there." —S.B.

"...your forms and directions are easy to follow." —C.V.M.

*Legal Survival Guides are directly available from the publisher, or from your local bookstores.*
*For credit card orders call 1–800–43–BRIGHT, write P.O. Box 372, Naperville, IL 60566,*
*or fax 630-961-2168*

# LEGAL SURVIVAL GUIDES™ NATIONAL TITLES
### *Valid in All 50 States*

### LEGAL SURVIVAL IN BUSINESS

| | |
|---|---|
| How to Form Your Own Corporation (2E) | $19.95 |
| How to Register Your Own Copyright (2E) | $19.95 |
| How to Register Your Own Trademark (2E) | $19.95 |
| Most Valuable Business Forms You'll Ever Need | $19.95 |
| Most Valuable Corporate Forms You'll Ever Need | $24.95 |
| Software Law (with diskette) | $29.95 |

### LEGAL SURVIVAL IN COURT

| | |
|---|---|
| Crime Victim's Guide to Justice | $19.95 |
| Debtors' Rights (2E) | $12.95 |
| Defend Yourself Against Criminal Charges | $19.95 |
| Grandparents' Rights | $19.95 |
| Help Your Lawyer Win Your Case | $12.95 |
| Jurors' Rights | $9.95 |
| Legal Malpractice and Other Claims Against Your Lawyer | $18.95 |
| Legal Research Made Easy | $14.95 |
| Simple Ways to Protect Yourself From Lawsuits | $24.95 |
| Victim's Rights | $12.95 |
| Winning Your Personal Injury Claim | $19.95 |

### LEGAL SURVIVAL IN REAL ESTATE

| | |
|---|---|
| How to Buy a Condominium or Townhome | $16.95 |
| How to Negotiate Real Estate Contracts (2E) | $16.95 |
| How to Negotiate Real Estate Leases (2E) | $16.95 |
| Successful Real Estate Brokerage Management | $19.95 |

### LEGAL SURVIVAL IN PERSONAL AFFAIRS

| | |
|---|---|
| How to File Your Own Bankruptcy (4E) | $19.95 |
| How to File Your Own Divorce (3E) | $19.95 |
| How to Make Your Own Will | $12.95 |
| How to Write Your Own Living Will | $9.95 |
| Living Trusts and Simple Ways to Avoid Probate | $19.95 |
| Neighbor vs. Neighbor | $12.95 |
| Power of Attorney Handbook (2E) | $19.95 |
| Social Security Benefits Handbook | $14.95 |
| U.S.A. Immigration Guide (2E) | $19.95 |
| Guia de Inmigracion a Estados Unidos | $19.95 |

*Legal Survival Guides are directly available from the publisher, or from your local bookstores.*

*For credit card orders call 1–800–43–BRIGHT, write P.O. Box 372, Naperville, IL 60566, or fax 630-961-2168*

# LEGAL SURVIVAL GUIDES™ STATE TITLES

*Up-to-date for Your State*

## NEW YORK

| | |
|---|---|
| How to File for Divorce in NY | $19.95 |
| How to Make a NY Will | $12.95 |
| How to Start a Business in NY | $16.95 |
| How to Win in Small Claims Court in NY | $14.95 |
| Landlord's Rights and Duties in NY | $19.95 |
| New York Power of Attorney Handbook | $12.95 |

## PENNSYLVANIA

| | |
|---|---|
| How to File for Divorce in PA | $19.95 |
| How to Make a PA Will | $12.95 |
| How to Start a Business in PA | $16.95 |
| Landlord's Rights and Duties in PA | $19.95 |

## FLORIDA

| | |
|---|---|
| Florida Power of Attorney Handbook | $9.95 |
| How to Change Your Name in FL (3E) | $14.95 |
| How to File a FL Construction Lien (2E) | $19.95 |
| How to File a Guardianship in FL | $19.95 |
| How to File for Divorce in FL (4E) | $21.95 |
| How to Form a Nonprofit Corp in FL (3E) | $19.95 |
| How to Form a Simple Corp in FL (3E) | $19.95 |
| How to Make a FL Will (4E) | $9.95 |
| How to Modify Your FL Divorce Judgement (3E) | $22.95 |
| How to Probate an Estate in FL (2E) | $24.95 |
| How to Start a Business in FL (4E) | $16.95 |
| How to Win in Small Claims Court in FL (5E) | $14.95 |
| Land Trusts in FL (4E) | $24.95 |
| Landlord's Rights and Duties in FL (6E) | $19.95 |
| Women's Legal Rights in FL | $19.95 |

## GEORGIA

| | |
|---|---|
| How to File for Divorce in GA (2E) | $19.95 |
| How to Make a GA Will (2E) | $9.95 |
| How to Start and Run a GA Business (2E) | $18.95 |

## ILLINOIS

| | |
|---|---|
| How to File for Divorce in IL | $19.95 |
| How to Make an IL Will | $9.95 |
| How to Start a Business in IL | $16.95 |

## MASSACHUSETTS

| | |
|---|---|
| How to File for Divorce in MA | $19.95 |
| How to Make a MA Will | $9.95 |
| How to Probate an Estate in MA | $19.95 |
| How to Start a Business in MA | $16.95 |
| Landlord's Rights and Duties in MA | $19.95 |

## MICHIGAN

| | |
|---|---|
| How to File for Divorce in MI | $19.95 |
| How to Make a MI Will | $9.95 |
| How to Start a Business in MI | $16.95 |

## MINNESOTA

| | |
|---|---|
| How to File for Divorce in MN | $19.95 |
| How to Form a Simple Corporation in MN | $19.95 |
| How to Make a MN Will | $9.95 |
| How to Start a Business in MN | $16.95 |

## NORTH CAROLINA

| | |
|---|---|
| How to File for Divorce in NC | $19.95 |
| How to Make a NC Will | $9.95 |
| How to Start a Business in NC | $16.95 |

## TEXAS

| | |
|---|---|
| How to File for Divorce in TX | $19.95 |
| How to Form a Simple Corporation in TX | $19.95 |
| How to Make a TX Will | $9.95 |
| How to Probate an Estate in TX | $19.95 |
| How to Start a Business in TX | $16.95 |
| How to Win in Small Claims Court in TX | $14.95 |
| Landlord's Rights and Duties in TX | $19.95 |

*Legal Survival Guides are directly available from the publisher, or from your local bookstores.*

*For credit card orders call 1–800–43–BRIGHT, write P.O. Box 372, Naperville, IL 60566, or fax 630-961-2168*

# Legal Survival Guides™ • Order Form

| BILL TO: | | | SHIP TO: | |
|---|---|---|---|---|
| | | | | |
| **Phone #** | **Terms** | **F.O.B.** Chicago, IL | | **Ship Date** |

**Charge my:**

*VISA*  ☐ VISA   *MasterCard*  ☐ Mastercard   *AMERICAN EXPRESS*  ☐ American Express

☐ **Money Order** (no personal checks please)

Credit Card Number    Expiration Date

| Qty | ISBN | Title | Retail |
|---|---|---|---|
| | | **Legal Survival Guides Fall 97 National Frontlist** | |
| | 1-57071-223-9 | How to File Your Own Bankruptcy (4E) | $19.95 |
| | 1-57071-224-7 | How to File Your Own Divorce (3E) | $19.95 |
| | 1-57071-227-1 | How to Form Your Own Corporation (2E) | $19.95 |
| | 1-57071-228-X | How to Make Your Own Will | $12.95 |
| | 1-57071-225-5 | How to Register Your Own Copyright (2E) | $19.95 |
| | 1-57071-226-3 | How to Register Your Own Trademark (2E) | $19.95 |
| | | **Fall 97 New York Frontlist** | |
| | 1-57071-184-4 | How to File for Divorce in NY | $19.95 |
| | 1-57071-183-6 | How to Make a NY Will | $12.95 |
| | 1-57071-185-2 | How to Start a Business in NY | $16.95 |
| | 1-57071-187-9 | How to Win in Small Claims Court in NY | $14.95 |
| | 1-57071-186-0 | Landlord's Rights and Duties in NY | $19.95 |
| | 1-57071-188-7 | New York Power of Attorney Handbook | $12.95 |
| | | **Fall 97 Pennsylvania Frontlist** | |
| | 1-57071-177-1 | How to File for Divorce in PA | $19.95 |
| | 1-57071-176-3 | How to Make a PA Will | $12.95 |
| | 1-57071-178-X | How to Start a Business in PA | $16.95 |
| | 1-57071-179-8 | Landlord's Rights and Duties in PA | $19.95 |
| | | **Legal Survival Guides National Backlist** | |
| | 1-57071-166-6 | Crime Victim's Guide to Justice | $19.95 |
| | 1-57248-023-8 | Debtors' Rights (2E) | $12.95 |
| | 1-57071-162-3 | Defend Yourself Against Criminal Charges | $19.95 |
| | 1-57248-001-7 | Grandparents' Rights | $19.95 |
| | 0-913825-99-9 | Guia de Inmigracion a Estados Unidos | $19.95 |
| | 1-57248-021-1 | Help Your Lawyer Win Your Case | $12.95 |
| | 1-57071-164-X | How to Buy a Condominium or Townhome | $16.95 |
| | 1-57248-035-1 | How to Negotiate Real Estate Contracts (2E) | $16.95 |
| | 1-57248-036-X | How to Negotiate Real Estate Leases (2E) | $16.95 |
| | 1-57071-167-4 | How to Write Your Own Living Will | $9.95 |
| | 1-57248-031-9 | Jurors' Rights | $9.95 |
| | 1-57248-032-7 | Legal Malpractice and Other Claims Against Your Lawyer | $18.95 |
| | 1-57248-008-4 | Legal Research Made Easy | $14.95 |
| | 1-57248-019-X | Living Trusts and Simple Ways to Avoid Probate | $19.95 |
| | 1-57248-022-X | Most Valuable Business Forms You'll Ever Need | $19.95 |
| | 1-57248-007-6 | Most Valuable Corporate Forms You'll Ever Need | $24.95 |
| | 0-913825-41-7 | Neighbor vs. Neighbor | $12.95 |
| | 1-57248-044-0 | Power of Attorney Handbook (2E) | $19.95 |
| | 1-57248-020-3 | Simple Ways to Protect Yourself From Lawsuits | $24.95 |
| | 1-57248-033-5 | Social Security Benefits Handbook | $14.95 |
| | 1-57071-163-1 | Software Law (w/diskette) | $29.95 |
| | 0-913825-86-7 | Successful Real Estate Brokerage Mgmt. | $19.95 |
| | 1-57248-000-9 | U.S.A. Immigration Guide (2E) | $19.95 |
| | 0-913825-82-4 | Victim's Rights | $12.95 |
| | 1-57071-165-8 | Winning Your Personal Injury Claim | $19.95 |
| | | **Florida Backlist** | |
| | 0-913825-81-6 | Florida Power of Attorney Handbook | $9.95 |
| | 1-57248-028-9 | How to Change Your Name in FL (3E) | $14.95 |
| | 0-913825-84-0 | How to File a FL Construction Lien (2E) | $19.95 |
| | 0-913825-53-0 | How to File a Guardianship in FL | $19.95 |
| | 1-57248-046-7 | How to File for Divorce in FL (4E) | $21.95 |

| Qty | ISBN | Title | Retail |
|---|---|---|---|
| | | **Florida Backlist (cont')** | |
| | 1-57248-004-1 | How to Form a Nonprofit Corp in FL (3E) | $19.95 |
| | 0-913825-96-4 | How to Form a Simple Corp in FL (3E) | $19.95 |
| | 1-57248-027-0 | How to Make a FL Will (4E) | $9.95 |
| | 1-57248-056-4 | How to Modify Your FL Divorce Judgement (3E) | $22.95 |
| | 1-57248-003-3 | How to Probate an Estate in FL (2E) | $24.95 |
| | 1-57248-005-X | How to Start a Business in FL (4E) | $16.95 |
| | 0-913825-97-2 | How to Win in Small Claims Court in FL (5E) | $14.95 |
| | 1-57248-029-7 | Land Trusts in FL (4E) | $24.95 |
| | 1-57248-057-2 | Landlord's Rights and Duties in FL (6E) | $19.95 |
| | 0-913825-73-5 | Women's Legal Rights in FL | $19.95 |
| | | **Georgia Backlist** | |
| | 1-57248-058-0 | How to File for Divorce in GA (2E) | $19.95 |
| | 1-57248-047-5 | How to Make a GA Will (2E) | $9.95 |
| | 1-57248-026-2 | How to Start and Run a GA Business (2E) | $18.95 |
| | | **Illinois Backlist** | |
| | 1-57248-042-4 | How to File for Divorce in IL | $19.95 |
| | 1-57248-043-2 | How to Make an IL Will | $9.95 |
| | 1-57248-041-6 | How to Start a Business in IL | $16.95 |
| | | **Massachusetts Backlist** | |
| | 1-57248-051-3 | How to File for Divorce in MA | $19.95 |
| | 1-57248-050-5 | How to Make a MA Will | $9.95 |
| | 1-57248-053-X | How to Probate an Estate in MA | $19.95 |
| | 1-57248-054-8 | How to Start a Business in MA | $16.95 |
| | 1-57248-055-6 | Landlord's Rights and Duties in MA | $19.95 |
| | | **Michigan Backlist** | |
| | 1-57248-014-9 | How to File for Divorce in MI | $19.95 |
| | 1-57248-015-7 | How to Make a MI Will | $9.95 |
| | 1-57248-013-0 | How to Start a Business in MI | $16.95 |
| | | **Minnesota Backlist** | |
| | 1-57248-039-4 | How to File for Divorce in MN | $19.95 |
| | 1-57248-040-8 | How to Form a Simple Corporation in MN | $19.95 |
| | 1-57248-037-8 | How to Make a MN Will | $9.95 |
| | 1-57248-038-6 | How to Start a Business in MN | $16.95 |
| | | **North Carolina Backlist** | |
| | 0-913825-94-8 | How to File for Divorce in NC | $19.95 |
| | 0-913825-92-1 | How to Make a NC Will | $9.95 |
| | 0-913825-93-X | How to Start a Business in NC | $16.95 |
| | | **Texas Backlist** | |
| | 0-913825-91-3 | How to File for Divorce in TX | $19.95 |
| | 1-57248-009-2 | How to Form a Simple Corporation in TX | $19.95 |
| | 0-913825-89-1 | How to Make a TX Will | $9.95 |
| | 1-57248-010-6 | How to Probate an Estate in TX | $19.95 |
| | 0-913825-90-5 | How to Start a Business in TX | $16.95 |
| | 1-57248-012-2 | How to Win in Small Claims Court in TX | $14.95 |
| | 1-57248-011-4 | Landlord's Rights and Duties in TX | $19.95 |
| | | | |
| | | **SUBTOTAL** | |
| | | IL Residents add 6.75%, FL Residents add county sales tax | |
| | | Shipping— $4.00 for 1st book, $1.00 each additional | |
| | | **Total** | |

To order, call Sourcebooks at 1-800-43-BRIGHT or FAX (630)961-2168 (Bookstores, libraries, wholesalers—please call for discount)